The Blackberry Hollow
CUDDLY TOY BOOK

Valerie Janitch

A DAVID & CHARLES CRAFT BOOK

My thanks . . .

Very specially to Melvin Grey; first for bringing the
Hollow to life — and then for capturing it all with his
magic camera.

To my editor, Vivienne Wells, for helping me to
discover Blackberry Hollow.

To Dainty Toys, Unit 35, Phoenix Rd, Crowther
Industrial Estate, (District 3), Washington, Tyne and
Wear NE38 0AB (Tel: (091) 416 7886/417 6277) for
variety, quality and speedy delivery, particularly of fur
fabric.

To Albina and Henry Cooper OBE, for advising
Harvey Mouse on his golfing equipment.

To Cheryl Grey for helping Mrs Hedgehog
make her buns.

To Jeff Lewis, for his special lettering; and
Brian Osborne for the Hollow Oak signboard.

And to Jenny and Becky Osborne, for always being
there when I needed them.

**Details of other books and patterns by
Valerie Janitch can be obtained by writing to her at:
15 Ledway Drive, Wembley Park, Middlesex HA9 9TH.
Please enclose a stamped self-addressed envelope.**

Photographs by Melvin Grey
Artwork by Eadanart

Text, photographs & illustrations © Valerie Janitch 1989

British Library Cataloguing in Publication Data
Janitch, Valerie
    The Blackberry Hollow cuddly toy book.
    1. Soft toys. Making – Manuals
    I. Title
    745.592′4

ISBN 0-7153-9341-3

Typeset by ABM Typographics Ltd, Hull
and printed in West Germany
by Mohndruck GmbH

for David & Charles Publishers plc
Brunel House   Newton Abbot   Devon

Distributed in the United States by
Sterling Publishing Co Inc,
2 Park Avenue, New York, NY 10016

Contents

Introduction to Blackberry Hollow

Blackberry Hollow is anywhere and everywhere — and nowhere in particular. So you're quite likely to come across it one day. But even if you wait until the sun goes down and you've missed your tea, you probably won't see a single occupant. The creatures who live there are very private, and they object to visitors trampling down the bracken and poking careless toes through their front doors.

Much better to stay at home and thread your needle. Then, with fur fabric and felt, you can re-create the magic of Blackberry Hollow for yourself and those you love. Exclusive colour photographs reveal for the first time what life is really like in the Hollow: the Rabbits' christening party; Professor Barnowl's high school; Stationmaster Squirrel seeing all the Harvest Mice off on holiday; the Hedgehog family's new baby; Silvery Grey marrying Barleycorn Brown; the Hallowe'en fancy dress ball; Grandma and Grandpa Squirrel's golden wedding; the little ones' Christmas party. And there are the Blackberry Hollow Pixies too; swindled out of their savings by a wicked witch, they are trying to earn enough money to buy a television set.

All the characters — adults, children and babies — are here as actual-size patterns with detailed directions and diagrams. If you've never made a cuddly toy before, Blackberry Hollow is the place to start. But if you're already a dedicated toymaker, you'll discover a wealth of original new designs for toys and mascots — quick to make — and quick to sell, too!

HOW TO USE THIS BOOK

The best way to begin is to fall in love. Simply turn the pages of the book, pausing to study each picture, and wait for it to happen. If it doesn't, you'll just have to start again and choose a toy in the conventional way; that is, the most suitable subject for the purpose you require.

Some are ideal to sit in the cradle awaiting the arrival of a new baby. Many more are designed to share the rough-and-tumble life of a toddler learning to talk, or as comforting companions for small children tucked up in bed on a dark night. Whilst others double as cheerful mascot characters designed to capture the heart of anyone, young or old, and become a treasured friend with very special meaning.

Apart from the owls, all the animals are dressed as the characters they represent. But if you simply want to make a cuddly bunny or squirrel — even cuddly hedgehogs are possible in Blackberry Hollow! — just go for the basic toy, and stop there.

When you have decided which one to make, find the appropriate page and follow the instructions given there. You'll probably have to turn to the end of the book for the basic toy, then return to the original page to dress it. But not always — or there may be special instructions. So do check first.

After that, it's only a step to creating your own characters. You can interchange the garment patterns for the rabbits and the squirrels, making the appropriate adjustment for the tail. The mole is a little fatter, so alter the width of patterns as necessary.

The directions are numbered step by step; always read through the whole step, even though it may contain several operations. This will give you a clear picture of what you are aiming to achieve, and make each stage easier to understand.

There is also another dimension to this book. As in my two previous titles, *The Kate Greenaway Doll Book* and *The Fairytale Doll Book,* there are no copyright restrictions on the patterns, as long as you are planning to produce the toys personally, and therefore in limited numbers. Once again this is a response to all those readers who have written to ask my permission to use my designs because they wish to sell their work, either for fund-raising or for personal profit. All the toys are quick and easy to make — with the individuality and character which you need in the competitive world of selling your work. The patterns are all there for you to choose from — and you don't have to ask. You simply have to plan how much time and money you can afford to spend on making up the toy, so that you can offer it at a realistic price.

Take a few minutes off to read the stories. You might even decide to make the pixies too! They're amusing little characters and fun to use as a Christmas or party decoration. But *all* the toys in this book are designed for fun. So don't waste any more time; turn to the photographs and start falling in love . . .

BE PREPARED

You should find all the equipment you need already in your sewing basket. But check that it is in good condition; rusty pins, bent needles and blunt scissors take all the joy out of sewing — and spoil the results, too.

You'll need plenty of pins (easy-to-spot coloured glass-headed ones are a sensible precaution when working with fur fabric); a selection of needles, including a darner, and a tapestry needle for threading elastic (or you can use two tiny safety pins — fix one to each end); chalk, or coloured pencils, for marking. A small pair of tweezers, some pinking shears and a hole punch are all useful, but not essential.

Good scissors *are* essential; they should be sharp and well-aligned. A pair of small pointed ones is very important, to cut the fur fabric. Then a larger pair for other fabric and felt. A third pair, to cut your paper patterns, will avoid blunting your needlework scissors. A sharp craft knife is always useful — especially if you make Baby Hoggy's cradle (page 63). The OLFA, with snap-off blades, is ideal.

Your pattern-making equipment consists of a well-sharpened pencil, a ruler, a pair of compasses and plenty of household greaseproof paper. And you will need a sheet of graph paper to put underneath your tracing paper (or rule a large sheet of plain paper into squares, but make sure measurements are absolutely accurate).

Last but not least — adhesives. For most jobs, use a clear, quick-drying all-purpose adhesive like UHU, which has a long nozzle for easy application. But it's easier to stick fabric to card if you use a dry stick glue; some glue-sticks work only with paper, so check that the one you buy lists fabrics as well, such as UHU Stic.

MEASUREMENTS

Use either metric or imperial measurements, but don't compare the two because they are often different. To make the instructions as simple as possible for you, each design has been worked out individually in both metric and imperial, and the nearest most practical measurement is always given. It is important, therefore, that you use one set of measurements only.

When the direction of measurements is not specifically stated, the depth is given first, followed by the width — ie: 10 x 20cm (4 x 8in) = 10cm (4in) deep x 20cm (8in) wide.

MATERIALS

Fur fabric is obtainable from most department stores and smaller fabric shops, as well as some craft shops. However, you will often find a wider choice is available from mail order suppliers.

Coloured felts and fillings may be obtained from the same sources, but again, you will have a wider selection if you buy by mail order.

The other fabrics used are generally available from any store selling dress fabrics, although often the amounts needed are so small that you will be able to find what you need amongst the cuttings in your piece bag.

Most of the incidental items used are easy to find, and you will probably have many of them around the home already.

MAKE YOUR PATTERNS

Trace onto household greaseproof paper. When a pattern for fur or felt has a fold line, trace it onto folded paper; cut through the double thickness, then open it out to cut flat in single fabric. To make a pattern from a diagram, place your tracing paper over a sheet of graph paper or ruled squares; then use a ruler to measure and rule the lines. Add the name, and copy all the markings carefully.

To transfer a pattern to thin card or paper, trace it first onto greaseproof paper, then rub over the back with a soft pencil; fix this side flat on your card and retrace the lines with a firm point (ballpoint pen, hard pencil or knitting needle). Remove the trace, and a clear outline should remain on the card. (For patterns traced onto folded paper, turn the tracing over and trace your original outline through onto the other side before opening it up.)

The arrows on fabric patterns indicate the straight of the fabric; the arrow should be parallel to the selvedge when the pattern is pinned to the fabric. On fur fabric, the arrow also indicates the direction of the pile.

When a pattern piece is marked 're-verse', turn it over to cut the second piece. Check to ensure that stripes, checks, etc, match equally on both pieces.

File all your patterns in a stiff envelope-type folder (obtainable from stationery or office suppliers).

WORKING WITH FUR FABRIC

Sewing fur fabric is a delight! Even when you make minor mistakes or briefly forget your Sunday-best stitching . . . the chances are it just won't show. So your very first toy can look really professional. To ensure it has a long and happy life, invest in a good fur fabric; before buying it, study the photograph and read the directions.

Pin your pattern pieces on the back, which looks like knitted jersey; use the vertical lines for the straight of the fabric. And stroke the fur like a cat to feel the pile; then make sure it is running in the direction of the arrow on the pattern. If a pattern has to be cut twice (or four times), you may have to turn it over to cut the second piece. To avoid mistakes, it's a good idea to trace a pattern for *every* piece you need — ie two heads (reversing the second), four arms (reversing two) etc.

Use small, sharp, pointed scissors — and only cut the jersey back of the fabric, *not* the fur. Transfer all markings accurately, using a contrasting chalk pencil — or with a couple of stitches in coloured thread.

Seams of 5mm ($^3/_{16}$in) are allowed for the adult animals; slightly less for the smaller ones. Work with the right sides together unless otherwise indicated. Pin each seam before stitching, pushing any protruding pile down between the two layers of fabric. Using a medium-size needle and your favourite regular-weight thread, sew with a back-stitch. Don't clip the seams before turning. Afterwards release any pile caught in the seams by brushing it very firmly with a pin.

As you stuff, the fabric will stretch — creating the cuddly rounded shape which will give your toy its charm and character. Patient stuffing is the secret of success, so do spend time and care on it. Never try to economise on your choice of filling; foam chips or old tights spell disaster.

Use small pieces of good quality washable polyester filling, teasing it out before pushing it well down into noses, paws and feet, then adding the next bit. Use a long darning needle to move the stuffing around from outside. Don't under-stuff; remember your toy will be receiving a lot of love, and too much cuddling can leave *any-one* limp! So stuff quite firmly, unless otherwise directed, moulding smoothly from the outside. Make sure heads are well rounded, then add more filling to emphasise nose and chin.

Some animals have their heads sewn to their bodies with a LADDER STITCH. Place the head in position and, beginning at the back, make a stitch in the body, where you want the head to join it; then take your thread straight up and make a stitch in the head; take your thread straight down to make another stitch in the body — and up to make another stitch in the head. The thread between the stitches forms the ladder.

LADDER STITCH

When embroidering mouths, begin and end some distance away; when the mouth is finished, pull the ends of the thread taut and clip them off close to the fabric, so that they disappear inside. Snip away fur which actually hides mouth or eyes, but go gently, as it's easy to trim off too much.

SAFETY: Apart from the mole, all the toys have eyes and noses made from felt. But if you prefer manufactured features, always purchase safety eyes and noses — which are permanently locked in at the back. Button eyes are very dangerous, and must never be substituted.

CREATING CHARACTER

Just like everyone the world over, the clothes which the inhabitants of Blackberry Hollow wear say a lot about the kind of characters they are. Study the photographs and read the list of materials carefully. The fabric used for each item is always described in detail — and if you follow this guidance, you can't go wrong.

Medium-weight dress fabrics or sheeting are most often used; firmly and evenly woven cotton, cotton-blend or cotton-type. Avoid silky man-made fabrics, and also thick or knobbly ones; both will fray and be difficult to sew. When making blouses, bodices or shirts as part of the basic figure, it is especially important to choose a strong, firm fabric that can be joined to the fur and will stand up to stuffing. Bulky hems can spoil a garment; if possible, cut your fabric along the thread, then turn the hem under and herringbone-stitch over the raw edge.

Never economise when buying felt. Choose a good quality, which is smooth and firm, and of an even thickness all over. To join it, oversew (overcast) the edges very neatly with matching thread and tiny stitches; then press the seam flat with your fingernail.

It is much easier to cut very small felt circles accurately if you mark them directly onto the felt. Find something with a circular rim the size you require — a thimble, the top from a pill container, pen cap, etc — the sharper the edge the better. Rub a contrasting wax crayon, lead pencil, felt-tip pen or chalk liberally over the rim. Press down onto the felt; then, still pressing firmly, twist it like a pastry cutter, taking care not to move the position. Lift off and cut along the marked line with sharp scissors. Alternatively, find — or cut — a self-adhesive label the size of the circle you require; press it lightly down onto your felt, then cut round it. Remove the label carefully.

Finally, some readers may be shocked that the ladies of Blackberry Hollow aren't too bothered about underpinnings beneath their full skirts. If modesty demands a pair of pantalettes, use the pattern for fabric trousers (Grandpa and Filbert Speedwell — page 89): make them up in a medium-weight cotton-type fabric (ignoring the tail section if for a rabbit or mole), and trim lavishly with lace and ribbon. And if madam needs a petticoat as well, use the same fabric and follow the directions for the skirt, making it about 1cm (⅜in) shorter, and trimming to match the pantalettes.

Note: Pattern pieces are placed across the width of the fabric for cutting, so that if you are buying fabric, you will need to purchase the smallest possible amount. However, in case you are using a piece of fabric that you already have, the width quoted is not always an accepted loom width from selvedge to selvedge, but indicates the actual width of fabric needed.

TRIMMINGS AND DECORATION

A lace trim, a scrap of ribbon, a braided edge, a tiny flower . . . all help to shape the character you are creating. Fancy braids make a toy look very professional, and they also give a firm edge to garments made from felt. Try to find lightweight narrow dress or lampshade braids — or ones which can be cut down the centre to make *two* lengths of *very* narrow braid. If you can't find a narrow braid in the colour you want, plait ribbon to make your own.

Flowers can be quite expensive, so look out for cheap ones, and use them sparingly. Alternatively, you can make sensational roses — in anything from bud to full bloom — out of ribbon. Little tassels are fun — so are woolly pompons.

Coloured glass or shimmering pearl beads and glittering sequins are a quick and easy way to add a touch of romance and sparkle. But avoid them if the toy is for a small child, along with wooden beads, buttons, rings, chains and similar items which could be dangerous. These little touches often 'make' the character of a mascot figure. But their omission won't make any difference to a child's enjoyment of the toy; it will only protect their safety.

MAKE YOUR OWN TRIMMINGS

All the ribbon trims in this book are made from Offray ribbons. They offer a rainbow palette of wonderful shades — in a comprehensive range of widths. So you can be sure of always finding just the right colour to match or contrast with the item you are trimming.

RIBBON BOWS

The formal bow looks wonderfully elegant in a wide satin or gauzey ribbon; the butterfly bow, in any width, is as dainty as its name.

Formal Bows
1. Fold under the cut ends of your piece of ribbon (the directions will tell you the width and how long it should be), so that they overlap at the centre back (figure a).

2. Gather the centre (figure b) and draw up, binding tightly several times with your thread to hold it securely (figure c).

3. Fold a scrap of ribbon lengthways into three and bind it closely around the centre: secure the ends at the back and trim off the surplus (figure d).

RIBBON BOWS

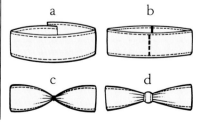

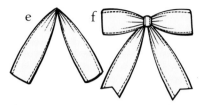

4. Gather across the centre of another piece of ribbon (length again as specified), then draw up tightly and fold it around as figure (e) for the ties (streamers).

5. Stitch the ties behind the bow and trim the cut ends in an inverted V-shape (figure f).

Butterfly Bows

1. Cut a piece of single-face satin ribbon (the directions will tell you the width and the length). On the wrong side, mark point A at the centre, close to the lower edge (figure g). On the right side, mark dots for points B on the top edge — see your individual directions for the distance points B should be from A. Then trim the cut ends in an inverted V-shape as figure h.

2. Hold the ribbon with the wrong side facing you. Using closely matching thread, bring your needle through point A from the back, close to the edge of the ribbon. Then curve the ends around and bring the needle through each point B. Draw up so that

both points B are over point A (figure i).

3. Make tiny gathering stitches up from points B to C (figure j). Take your thread over the top edge of the bow and gather right down from point C to point D. Draw up neatly, then wind the thread tightly around three or four times and secure at the back so that the result resembles figure k.

PLAITED BRAID

To make a very narrow, dainty braid, in exactly the shade you want, just plait together three lengths of Offray's 1.5mm (1/16in) wide satin ribbon. Or plait two or three different shades together to make a multi-coloured braid.

1. The directions for the item that you are making will usually tell you how much ribbon you need to make the length of braid you require. For instance: 'Make a plait from three 25cm (10in) lengths of 1.5mm (1/16in) ribbon.' In this case, if you are making the braid in one colour only, cut one 25cm (10in) length of ribbon and one 50cm (20in) length. Fold the longer piece in half, smear a trace of glue inside the fold, place one end of the shorter piece between the fold, then pinch together (figure a).

PLAITED BRAID

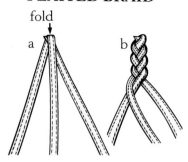

2. Push a pin through the folded end and secure it to a drawing-board or something similar. Then begin to plait very evenly, making sure that the strands of ribbon are always flat — never fold them over. Keep the ribbon taut and draw the plait very firmly between your fingertips every 2-3cm (inch or so) to make it smooth and even (figure b). Hold the ends together with a paper-clip.

3. Glue the braid into place, spreading the glue just beyond the point where you intend to cut it, to ensure that it does not unravel. Press the cut ends down well, adding a little more glue if necessary.

4. If you are not following directions, you can calculate the amount of ribbon needed by measuring the length of braid you require and adding a third (then multiply by three for the total amount). For example, if you need a 30cm (12in) length of braid, plait three pieces of ribbon 40cm (16in) long. If you want to make a multi-colour braid in two or three toning shades, divide the total amount by three to calculate the quantity of each ribbon.

SATIN ROSES

The width of the ribbon determines the size of the flower; the longer it is, the more petals it will have. The directions will indicate the width and length that you should use for the design. Use single-face satin ribbon (except for miniature 3mm (1/8in) roses).

1. Cut a length of ribbon as directed. Fold the corner as the broken line on figure a and bring point A down to

BUTTERFLY BOWS

g

| wrong side |
| A |

h

right side
A

B   B

i
A
B

j
C
B
D

k

meet point B as figure b. Fold again as the broken line on figure b and bring point C over point A to meet point B as figure c. (Omit the second fold for 3mm (1/8in) ribbon.)

2. Roll the ribbon round four times, with the folded corner inside, to form a tight tube, and make a few stitches through the base to hold (figure d). This forms the centre of the rose.

3. To make the petals, fold the ribbon down so that the edge is aligned with the tube (figure e), then curve the ribbon around the tube to form a cone, keeping the top of the tube level with the diagonal fold. When the tube again lies parallel to the remaining ribbon, make two or three stitches at the base to hold the petal you have just made (figure f).

4. Continue to make petals with the remainder of the ribbon, sewing each one to the base of the flower before you start the next (figure g). Shape the rose as you work by gradually making the petals a little more open.

5. Finish the cut end neatly underneath the base of the completed rose (figure h).

SATIN ROSES

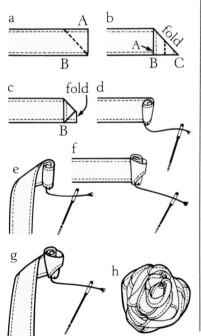

TINY TASSELS

1. Take a length of 1.5mm (1/16in) wide ribbon and fold it as instructed — the length and number of folds determine the size of the tassel. Your individual directions will tell you how much ribbon and how many lengths you will require.

2. Hold the folded ends neatly together and absolutely level (figure a), then make a knot at the centre (figure b). Take the two sides down so that all the ends are together, then bind very tightly with matching thread close under the knot (figure c).

3. Snip off the folded ends and trim neatly to length (figure d).

TINY TASSELS

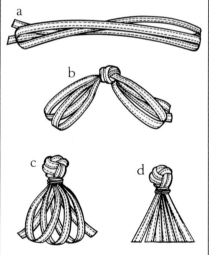

WOOLLY POMPONS

No self-respecting rabbit can do without one! They can be purchased in a variety of sizes . . . but the ones you make yourself are the best.

The directions are always the same; but the size of the card circle determines the size of your ball. This pattern makes a trimmed pompon about 4cm (1½in) in diameter. For a larger or smaller pompon, simply adjust the size of the pattern.

YOU WILL NEED:
Knitting yarn: most types will do, but avoid anything *very* thick or thin or heavily textured
Strong thread or fine string (if your yarn is not strong, see step 3)
Thin card
A large tapestry needle .
Small pointed scissors

1. Cut two circles of card as the pattern. Fold a 4m (4yd) length of yarn into four and thread a tapestry needle (have fewer strands if your yarn is thicker). Place the two card circles together and wrap the yarn evenly over and over them as figure a, continuing until the central hole is full (figure b).

2. Push pointed scissors through the yarn and between the two card circles (see the arrow on figure b). Cut the yarn all round (keeping your scissors between the card).

3. Slip a 20cm (8in) length of double yarn between the two layers of card to surround the yarn in the centre; knot together, pulling as tight as you can (use thread or string if your yarn is liable to break).

4. Cut away the card, then trim the pompon severely (but not the ties) to make a neat, round, firm ball.

5. Use the ties to fix the pompon in place — or snip them off if not needed.

WOOLLY POMPON

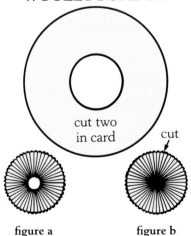

cut two in card

cut

figure a   figure b

Harriet Hemlock's Book of Spells

Flip stood at the door of Toadstool Cottage. He looked cross as a small figure hurried up Blackberry Lane.

Flop was out of breath; 'I met a witch!' he puffed. 'Her name is Harriet Hemlock, and she's offered to sell us her Book of Spells.'

'We can't buy it,' said Flip. 'We haven't any money.'

'But our money-box is nearly full,' Flop contradicted.

'That's for our television set!' shouted Flip.

Last winter they had been snowed up for weeks, with nothing to do but toast crumpets and read. So they were saving to buy a television.

Flop wondered how Flip could be so stupid. 'If we had the Book of Spells, we needn't buy a television set. Harriet Hemlock says there's a spell to turn a mushroom into a television set.'

The next day Harriet Hemlock came to tea. She wore a long black cloak, and was followed by a black cat with a very superior expression.

Flip wasn't impressed. 'Are you sure she's a witch?' he hissed as the old woman gobbled up the fruit cake and jam tarts. 'She eats a lot.'

'Even witches get hungry,' whispered Flop.

So they agreed to spend their savings on the Book of Spells. The cat grinned slyly as Harriet Hemlock tipped the coins into a bag.

Flip and Flop found an extra large mushroom in the woods. They put it in a bowl, with two stools in front, ready to sit and watch. The list of strange ingredients in the spell included a mouldy acorn, half a withered leaf, five blue feathers and some elderberry juice. They spent all day gathering everything and then used their biggest saucepan to boil the ingredients for two hours. When the mixture was cool, they poured it over the mushroom.

Flip and Flop sat excitedly watching the mushroom. Half-an-hour later they were still watching; the mushroom was still a mushroom. Flip sighed: 'I told you she wasn't a witch, her spells don't work.'

'Now we haven't any money we'll never have a television set,' wept Flop.

'We'll have to earn some,' said Flip. 'We'll start Pixie Enterprises, helping people whenever they need it.'

Flop stared miserably at the mushroom. Flip ignored him as he wrote out a poster saying: 'HELP! Call Pixie Enterprises (Flip and Flop) if you want a job done. Enything considered. Reesonable rates.' He put on his hat and went out to pin it to the Hollow Oak.

Then they sat down to await their first customer.

Posy-Rose Brown's Christening

Mrs Brown was sewing pink satin bows onto a lace trimmed christening gown. There was so much to do. Salads to make for the party afterwards. Her husband's trousers to press. And then there were the flower arrangements to do. She wanted lots of flowers for her daughter's christening.

'That's no problem,' said Mr Brown, 'Flip and Flop are looking for work. We'll ask them to do the flowers.'

It was their first job, and the two pixies were very excited. They worked hard, filling enormous baskets with colourful blooms and placing them near the font where the Reverend Mole would christen the baby.

When the guests arrived they all admired the pixies' flower baskets.

Then everyone was quiet because the service had begun. The Reverend Mole was reading from his prayer book. Mrs Rabbit nursed the baby dressed in her long robe. Mr Rabbit looked on proudly, and Barnabas tried to see how much water there was in the font.

Then the Reverend Mole sneezed. 'Excuse me,' he apologised, as he sneezed again, 'it's my hay fever.'

The noise woke the baby, and she began to cry.

'I get this terrible . . . a-tishoo! . . . hay fever,' the Reverend Mole explained, dabbing his eyes and nose and then putting his spectacles on again. 'The . . . a-choo! . . . pollen in the flowers brings it on . . . a-tishoo! Those pixies with their stupid . . . a-choo! . . . flowers. Quite unnecessary.' He turned to glare at Flip and Flop — who glared back — they thought it was most unfair to blame them.

'May I have the . . . a-tishoo! . . . baby, please,' said the Reverend Mole.

'I baptise this child . . .' he said, and there was a hushed silence as everyone held their breath: 'A-TISHOO!'

The guests gasped and looked at each other in horror. Mrs Brown burst into tears. The baby cried even more, and Barnabas got the giggles.

'I think,' Flip whispered to Flop, 'that we might as well go home.'

'Aren't we going to wait to be paid?' asked Flop.

'I'm afraid we'd be wasting our time,' Flip replied. 'I've a feeling we're not very popular here.'

MR BROWN

Father Rabbit

Father Rabbit wears a smart blue and white candy-stripe shirt under his jacket. So when you turn to the directions for the basic Adult Rabbit, follow the 'sleeve-and-paw' version. Tiny embroidered flower motifs are used here for his buttons, to make the toy suitable for a very young child. But if it is intended for an older child, or as an adult mascot, you could use either very tiny buttons, or coloured beads.

MATERIALS
*Antelope brown fur fabric, 23cm (9in) deep x 70cm (27in) wide or 40cm (16in) deep x 45cm (18in) wide
White fur fabric, 12cm (5in) deep x 23cm (9in) wide
Shirt, blouse or bodice fabric, 10cm (4in) deep x 60cm (24in) wide (see basic Adult Rabbit)
6.5 x 12.5cm (2½ x 5in) brown felt (to tone with fur)
5cm (2in) square black felt
Polyester stuffing
Stranded black embroidery cotton
White-pompon, 4cm (1½in) diameter for tail (if required) *or* fluffy white knitting yarn
Matching and black threads
Scraps of stiff card or plastic (double cereal carton or cottage cheese tub lid)
Clear adhesive*

20 x 22cm (8 x 8½in) green felt for trousers
10 x 15cm (4 x 6in) lilac felt for waistcoat (vest)
30cm (12in) square violet felt for jacket
10cm (4in) green/blue tartan taffeta ribbon, 16mm (⅝in) wide, for his bow-tie
3 tiny green embroidered flower motifs (or buttons or beads — see above)
Matching threads
Clear adhesive

1. Use the pattern pieces for the Adult Rabbit (pages 102-3). Cut the head gusset once, the leg twice and the paw and ear four times each (note direction of pile), all in brown fur fabric. Cut the face twice in white fur fabric, reversing the second piece. Cut the body and sleeve twice each in the shirt fabric. Cut the sole twice in felt; then cut it again slightly smaller, following the broken line, in card or stiff plastic. Mark notches. Leave the face pattern pinned to the fabric.

2. Turn to page 100 and follow the directions for the 'sleeve and-paw' version of the basic Adult Rabbit.

3. Make the ribbon into a formal bow (see Trimmings: page 7), but done bind the centre. Stitch to the shirt, close under his chin.

4. Cut Father Rabbit's trouser pattern twice in green felt. Oversew each piece together between a-b. Then join the two piece together between c-a-c, to form the centre front and back seams. Turn to the right side. Gather round the top edge, then fit trousers on rabbit and draw up round the waist, catching to the body to hold in position.

5. Cut the waistcoat (vest) in lilac felt. Stitch or glue flowers, buttons or beads down centre front.
    Place flat on the shirt front, taking the side edges (d-d) smoothly round and pinning them to the back of the body, just behind the seam. Take the top points of the waistcoat (e) over the shoulders and round the neck, pinning to the body just behind the head. Make sure the waistcoat fits very snugly, then stitch the sides and top pieces to the body, removing the pins.

6. Cut the jacket back once, and the front, sleeve and pocket flap twice each, in violet felt.
    Oversew the front pieces to the back at each shoulder (f-g).
    Gather the top edge of each sleeve between the circles. Fit the sleeves into the armholes, matching the side edges (h) and centre top to the shoulder seam (g). Draw up the gathers to fit, and stitch into place.
    Join the sleeve and side seams (j-h-k). Turn to the right side.
    Spread a little glue along the top edge of each pocket flap, then stick to the jacket as indicated on the pattern for the front.

7. Use either a purchased pompon, or make one (see Trimmings: page 9). Stitch or glue to back of trousers, over the seam.

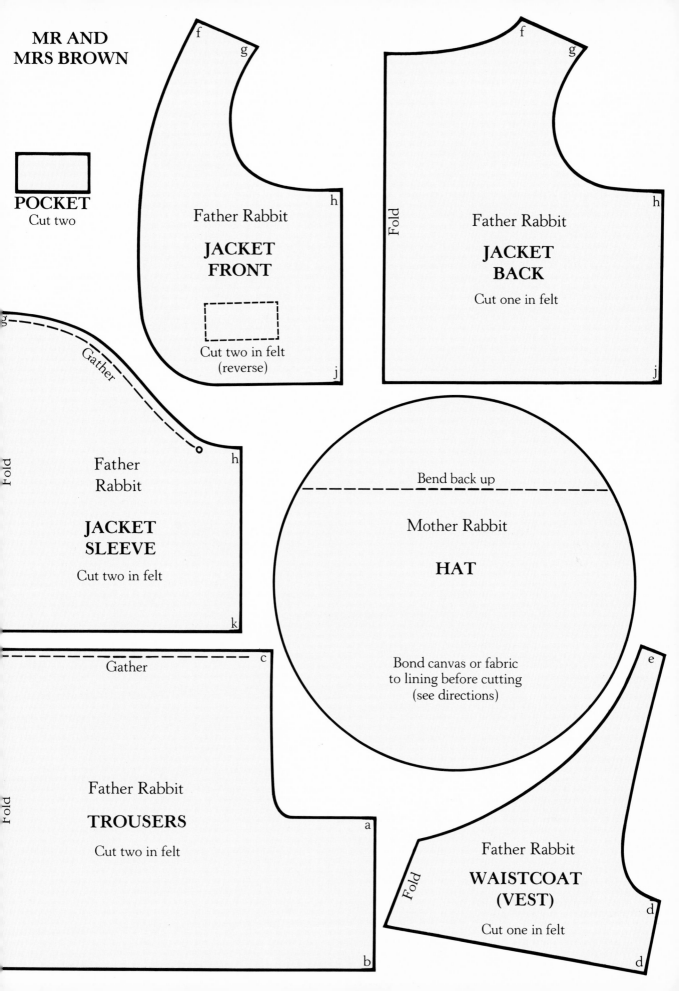

MR AND MRS BROWN

POCKET
Cut two

Father Rabbit
JACKET FRONT
Cut two in felt
(reverse)

f
g
h
j

Father Rabbit
JACKET BACK
Cut one in felt

Fold

f
g
h
j

Gather

g

Father Rabbit
JACKET SLEEVE
Cut two in felt

Fold

h
k

Gather

c

Bend back up

Mother Rabbit
HAT

Bond canvas or fabric
to lining before cutting
(see directions)

e

Father Rabbit
TROUSERS
Cut two in felt

Fold

a
b

Father Rabbit
WAISTCOAT (VEST)
Cut one in felt

Fold

d
d

MRS BROWN

Mother Rabbit

Tiny blue and lilac flowers on a pale blue ground were Mrs Brown's choice for her blouse, and this set the theme for her entire outfit. The plain blue skirt with an outsize satin bow at the back matches the forget-me-nots on her hat, and everything is daintily trimmed with lilac lace. It's fun to plan a colour scheme in this way, starting with one item and letting it dictate the rest.

MATERIALS

Materials to make the basic rabbit are exactly the same as for Mr Brown between * and * (see page 14)

14 x 60cm (5½ x 24in) blue medium-weight
   cotton-type fabric for her skirt
12cm (4½in) diameter circle of natural-colour fine
   canvas or buckram, or stiffened fabric, for her hat
12cm (4½in) diameter circle lilac satin or other fabric
   to line hat
12cm (4½in) iron-on bonding material or fusible
   webbing (Vilene Bondaweb)
25cm (¼yd) matching blue satin ribbon, 39mm
   (1½in) wide, for her sash
50cm (½yd) organdie ribbon, 23mm (⅞in) wide, for
   the hat
2m (2yd) lilac lace, 10-15mm (about ½in) deep
35cm (⅜yd) heavy lilac lace or narrow braid for the
   hat
Small bunch of forget-me-nots
A few small leaves (optional)
Matching threads
Clear adhesive

1. Use the pattern pieces for the Adult Rabbit (pages 102-3). Cut the head gusset once, the leg twice and the paw and ear four times each (note direction of pile), all in brown fur fabric. Cut the face twice in white fur fabric, reversing the second piece. Cut the body and sleeve twice each in the blouse fabric. Cut the sole twice in felt; then cut it again slightly smaller, following the broken line, in card or stiff plastic. Mark notches.

2. Turn to page 100 and follow the directions for the 'sleeve-and-paw' version of the basic Adult Rabbit (omitting the mouth).

When you have turned up the lower edge of the sleeve (step 11b), tack lace so that the straight edge covers about 3mm (⅛in) fabric, and the remainder overlaps below; gather the lace and fabric together, to form wrist frill.

The mouth is a single stitch, just under 1cm (⅜in) long, using six strands of black embroidery cotton, positioned exactly 1cm (⅜in) below the nose.

3. Join short edges of skirt fabric, for centre back seam, and press open. Turn to the right side.

4. Mark top edge into four; turn raw edge under and gather close to fold. Fit on rabbit and pin just above waist seam, marked points at sides and centre front. Draw up to fit and stitch, using double thread and a darning needle.

5. Turn up hem and stitch. Then trim with lace, over the stitching line.

6. Make a formal bow from blue ribbon (see Trimmings: page 7) and stitch at centre back of waist.

7. Bond lilac satin to underside of canvas, then cut the hat. Gather remaining lace and stitch to satin, overlapping edge of hat. Glue heavy lace or braid around top edge of hat.

8. Fold up back as indicated. Stitch hat to top of head, as illustrated, catching ears securely to the back.

9. Glue forget-me-nots and leaves on top. Make streamers (ties) (Formal Bows, step 4) from 30cm (12in) organdie ribbon and glue to back of hat to hang down between the ears. Make a formal bow from remaining ribbon and glue on top.

10. Make the baby as directed, then stitch securely in mother's arms.

POSY-ROSE BROWN

Baby Rabbit

A soft shade of brown, or a pale grey, are the best colours for the bunny babe. Very cheap, simple and quick-to-make, this could be a useful design if you want a tiny attraction to mass-produce for your bazaar stall.

Use left-over scraps of fabric to dress the babies, so that no two are identical: beg, borrow or steal cuttings from summer dress fabrics, especially if they are patterned with tiny flowers or have a similar dainty design. The petticoat fabric should be plain, but under the kind of cotton dress described above, a lightweight cotton would be as good, if not better than satin.

The tiny bows could be omitted, to speed up production — although just one tucked under the chin would be worth the extra effort. Fix a loop of very narrow ribbon behind the neck, so that they can be used as hanging mascots.

MATERIALS
18cm (7in) square of mid-brown felt
Scrap of black felt
6 x 7cm (2½ x 2¾in) iron-on bonding material (Vilene Bondaweb) or fusible webbing (or use clear adhesive)
Polyester stuffing
15 x 25cm (6 x 10in) cream medium-weight cotton dress fabric for the robe
15 x 18cm (6 x 7in) pink satin for the petticoat
30cm (12in) narrow cream lace, about 10mm (⅜in) deep
15cm (6in) narrow pink lace, about 10mm (⅜in) deep
50cm (½yd) pink satin ribbon, 3mm (⅛in) wide
Matching threads
Clear adhesive

1. Cut the head gusset and the body once, and the face (reversing the second piece) and ear twice, in felt. Bond or glue each ear to another piece of felt and trim away the surplus level with the cut edge so that they are double thickness.

2. Mark notches on the wrong side of the gusset. Mark a dot for the eye on the right side of each face piece.

3. Oversew the two face pieces together between a-b. Carefully match the tip of the gusset (a) to the top of the seam; then oversew it to each side of the face be-

tween a and the single notch. Join the other end of each seam, between c and the double notch. Now gather each side of the gusset between the single and double notches. Pin the gusset to the face at each side, drawing up the gathers as you do so and distributing them evenly along the length of the seam, easing the gusset in to fit round the top of the face. Oversew securely over the gathers. Turn to the right side.

4. Stuff the head well, moulding it into shape from the outside. Using a double thread, gather round the lower edge of the head, then draw up tightly and secure, leaving just a small hole no more than 1cm (⅜in) in diameter (before securing your thread, check that the head is sufficiently stuffed, adding more filling if necessary).

5. Join the side edges of the body to form the centre back seam. Gather round the lower edge, draw up as tightly as possible and secure. Turn to the right side and stuff. Gather round the top edge, draw up tightly and secure.

6. Take a stitch through the centre top of the body, from back to front, under the gathers. Then take a stitch across the hole under the head, from front to back; then repeat the first stitch through the body. Draw up, so that the head is in the correct position, then repeat to hold it in place. Now ladder stitch all round, alternately taking one stitch through the head and one through the body, securing them firmly together. Go round again, drawing your thread more tightly, if necessary.

7. Cut the pink satin following the diagram for the petticoat. Join the centre back seam and press it open. Stitch pink lace around the lower edge (don't turn up a hem unless you have to). Turn under the top edge and gather very close to the folded edge. Mark the centre front, then fit the petticoat over the body and draw up the gathers round the neck, matching centre front and back points. Catch securely to the rabbit's neck.

8. Make up the dress fabric in exactly the same way, following the diagram for the robe and trimming the

lower edge with cream lace; but before gathering the top, add a lace collar. To do this, pin the lace over the dress, the straight edge level with the folded top edge; then gather and draw up round the neck as for the petticoat.

9. Make eight butterfly bows from 5cm (2in) lengths of ribbon (see Trimmings: page 8: points B are 1.5cm (⅝in) from A). Stitch one immediately under the chin, with the others at 2cm (¾in) intervals down the centre front of the robe.

10. Pin the ears to the back of the head, following the illustration; then stitch into place between the bottom point and the notch at each side.

11. Cut the eyes and nose in black felt (use a hole punch if you have one). Glue the eyes over the marked points and the nose at point a, where the gusset joins the two face pieces.

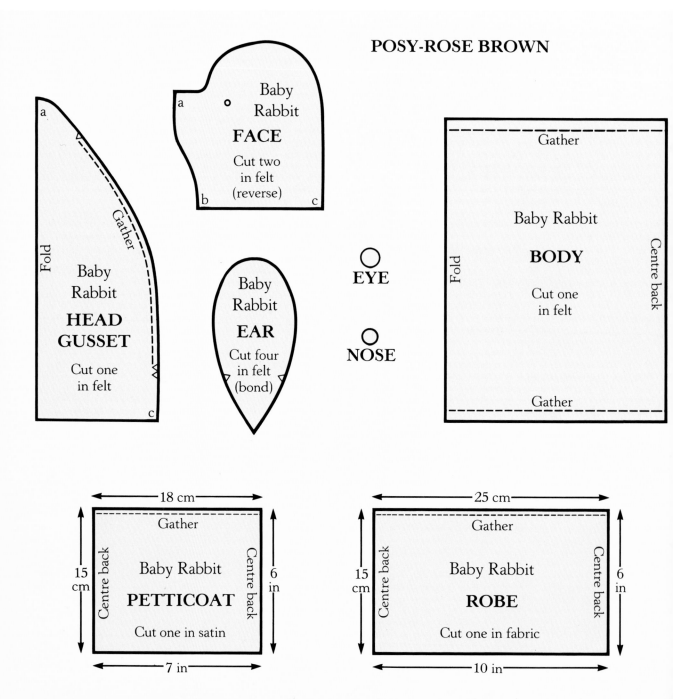

POSY-ROSE BROWN

BARNABAS BROWN

Young Barnabas Brown is always climbing in and out of mischief. His sporty shirt is a small gingham check: so this is another 'sleeve-and-paw' version of the basic directions. And it's never long before Barnabas comes through the knees of his sturdy dungarees, but when it happens his mother just sighs and sews on some cheerful patches — so that he looks like his friend, Frisky Speedwell (see page 93).

MATERIALS

Antelope brown fur fabric, 25cm (10in) deep x 30cm (12in) wide
8 x 15cm (3 x 6in) white fur fabric
15 x 20cm (6 x 8in) shirt fabric
5 x 10cm (2 x 4in) brown felt (to tone with fur)
3cm (1¼in) square black felt
Polyester stuffing
Stranded black embroidery cotton (optional)
Matching threads
Scraps of stiff card or plastic (double cereal carton or cottage cheese tub lid)
Clear adhesive

15cm (6in) square felt for dungarees
White pompon, 3cm (1¼in) diameter
  or fluffy white knitting yarn, for tail
Matching threads
Clear adhesive (as above)

1. Use the pattern pieces for the Junior Rabbit (page 104). Cut the head gusset once, the leg twice and the paw and ear four times each (note direction of pile), all in brown fur fabric. Cut the face twice in white fur fabric, reversing the second piece. Cut the body and sleeve twice each in the shirt fabric. Cut the sole twice in felt: then cut it again slightly smaller, following the broken line, in card or stiff plastic. Mark notches.

2. Turn to page 100 and follow the directions for the 'sleeve-and-paw' version of the basic Adult Rabbit, omitting the smiling mouth (step 2). Barnabas's mouth is a single stitch, about 8mm (5/16in) long, using six strands of embroidery cotton, positioned 8mm (5/16in) below the nose.

3. In felt, cut the dungarees leg twice, the bib once, and two straps, about 6mm (¼in) wide by 10cm (4in) long.

4. Oversew each leg together between a-b. Then join the two pieces between c-a-c, to form the centre front and back seams. Turn to the right side.

5. Matching the top of the centre front seam (c) to the notch at the centre of the lower edge of the bib, over-sew the two together. Glue one end of each strap behind the top corners of the bib (d), extending as indicated by the arrows.

6. Gather the waist edge, beginning and ending at each side of the bib.

7. Fit dungarees on rabbit, taking the straps over the shoulders and crossing them at the back before catching the ends to the back of the figure at waist level about 3cm (1¼in) apart: snip off any excess. Draw up the gathers to fit, catching the dungarees to the figure to hold in position.

8. If you haven't a purchased pompon, make one (see Trimmings: page 9). Glue to back of dungarees, over the seam.

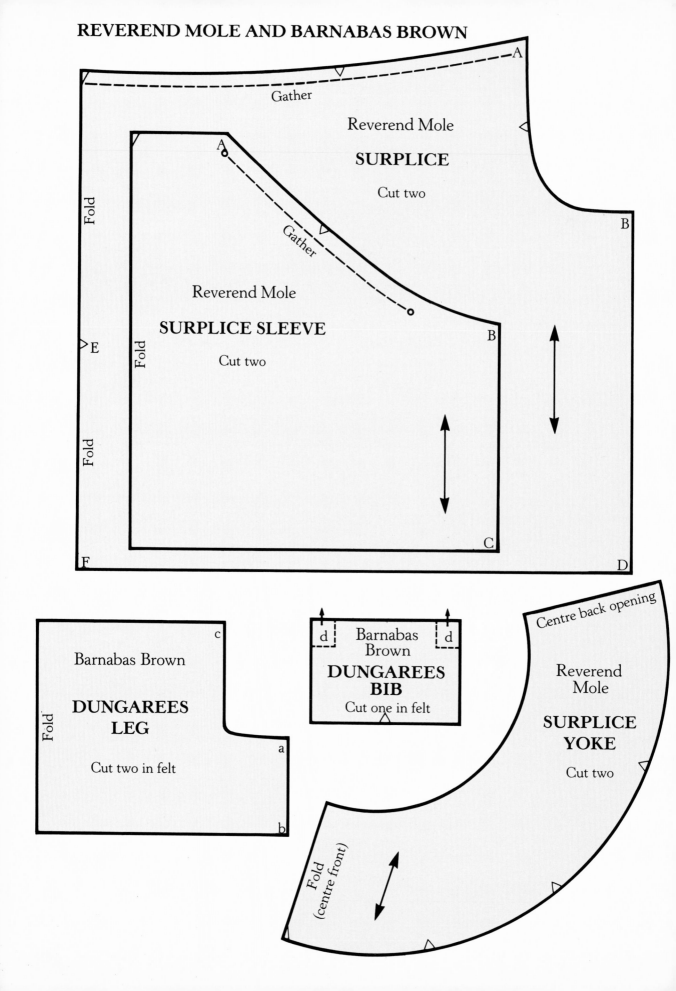

REVEREND MOLE AND BARNABAS BROWN

Gather

A

Reverend Mole

SURPLICE

Cut two

B

Fold

A

Fold

Gather

Reverend Mole

SURPLICE SLEEVE

Cut two

E

B

Fold

C

F

D

Barnabas Brown

DUNGAREES LEG

Cut two in felt

Fold

c

a

b

d

Barnabas Brown

DUNGAREES BIB

Cut one in felt

d

Centre back opening

Reverend Mole

SURPLICE YOKE

Cut two

Fold (centre front)

THE REVEREND MOLE

Use an opaque white fabric for his surplice: a cotton-blend is best, so that it won't crease too easily. Search for a suitably embroidered ribbon for his stole. And don't forget his pince-nez — or he won't be able to read the blessing!

First turn to page 109 to make the basic Adult Mole; then continue below.

MATERIALS

30cm (12in) medium-weight white cotton-blend fabric, 90cm (36in) wide
40cm (½yd) embroidered ribbon, 2-2.5cm (¾-1in) wide, for stole
2 snap fasteners
Matching thread
2 gilt curtain rings, 2cm (¾in) diameter
Gilt picture wire (or gold round elastic or cord)

1. Cut the surplice, sleeve and yoke twice each. Cut *one* surplice piece only in half along the fold line to form the two back pieces. Mark notches.

2. Gather both sides of each sleeve between the circles. Pin each sleeve to the front and back of the surplice along the armhole edges, matching points A-B: draw up the gathers to fit and stitch.

3. Join the side and sleeve seams C-B-D. Turn to the right side.

4. Beginning and ending 1cm (⅜in) from the centre back edges, gather all round the top edge of the surplice, including the sleeves.

Right sides together and raw edges level, pin the gathered edge around the outer edge of one yoke piece, matching centre back edges and notches. Draw up to fit and stitch.

Right sides together, stitch the second yoke piece to the first, along the inner edge and the centre back edges. Clip the corners and cut the seam into V-shaped notches all round the top of the yoke.

Turn the yoke to the right side, then turn the raw lower edge of the second yoke piece under and slip-stitch over the gathers on the inside of the surplice.

5. Join the back edges between E-F, then turn under and herringbone-stitch the raw edges above for centre back opening.

Stitch snap fasteners at top and bottom corners of the yoke to close centre back opening.

6. Turn under a narrow hem (about 6-7mm/¼in) around the sleeves and lower edge, and herringbone-stitch over the raw edge.

7. Press carefully before fitting on the mole.

8. Fringe the ends of the ribbon, then drape around his shoulders as illustrated.

9. Join the curtain rings with a short length of picture wire twisted between them, to hold them about 1cm (⅜in) apart. Then stitch the rings so that they perch on top of the nose as illustrated. (Alternatively, use gold elastic or cord and make as directed for Grandpa Speedwell: page 90 — step **5**.)

Trouble at Hollow Oak High School

Someone was sobbing. Mistress Barnowl peered down through the branches of the great tree. A small bundle of feathers stood trembling below. The schoolmistress swooped down and put her big wing round the baby owl.

'What is the matter, Fluff?' she asked.

Comforted by the warmth of her down, the little owl told her. 'I was crossing Blackberry Lane on my way to school,' he sniffed, 'when Barnabas Brown came round the corner on his scooter and nearly knocked me down.'

Mistress Barnowl tutted. Then she gave Fluff another cuddle before taking him to the branch where his classmates were waiting for lessons to begin. 'Look after him. He's had a nasty shock,' she told them. 'I must see the headmaster.'

Professor Barnowl was most concerned. 'Blackberry Lane is very dangerous,' he agreed. 'We need a lollipop man to see the pupils safely across. But where could we find one?'

'Flip and Flop are looking for work,' suggested Mistress Barnowl. 'We could ask them.'

The pixies were thrilled when they were asked to be lollipop men.

'I love making sweets,' said Flop, as they boiled the sugar syrup until it was thick, and then added bright colours. They poured it into little cups and stuck a stick into each. When the lollipops were hard, the pixies wrapped them in shiny paper and laid them in a big basket. Then they put on their hats and hurried down the lane.

Professor Barnowl looked at the clock. 'Ten minutes to four,' he muttered, 'I hope Flip and Flop are ready with their lollipop board.'

He was startled by Mistress Barnowl flying down from an upper branch.

'Those pixies!' she exploded, 'they've given all the children sticky sweets to suck. Now their feathers are in a dreadful mess — and most of the little ones are feeling sick.'

'But I didn't tell them to make sweets,' the headmaster gasped.

Mistress Barnowl glared at him: 'I think they misunderstood.'

Poor Mistress Barnowl was exhausted by the time she had washed and brushed all the sticky owls. When they were clean and feeling better the headmaster took them across Blackberry Lane and told them to hurry home.

Back in Toadstool Cottage Flip and Flop washed up their saucepans.

'They were such beautiful lollipops,' sighed Flop. 'The little owls loved them.'

'The headmaster didn't,' said Flip glumly.

'I think he was upset because we didn't offer him one,' decided Flop.

PROFESSOR AND MISTRESS

BARNOWL

No-one disputes the fact that Professor Barnowl is a wise old bird. But he finds that his mortar board not only reminds his pupils how very learned he is — it also helps him to keep his thoughts together. And if the little owls are over-awed by the formidable professor, Mistress Barnowl will always take them under her wing and give them a little cuddle.

First turn to page 113 to make up the basic Adult Owls. Then add his mortar board and her cap and apron, as described below.

PROFESSOR BARNOWL'S MORTAR BOARD

MATERIALS
18 x 26cm (7 x 10in) black felt
Medium-weight card (cereal carton)
Black silk tassel, 8cm (3in) long
50cm (½yd) black satin ribbon, 1.5mm (⅛in) wide
Black felt pen (or black ink, etc)
Dry-stick adhesive (optional)
Clear adhesive

1. Cut the card for the two top pieces and the side once each, cutting a hole in the centre of one top piece as indicated. Cut the felt side once.

2. Using the glue stick, cover one side of each top piece with felt, trimming it level with both the inner and outer edges.

3. Glue the strip of card for the side on top of the felt side, positioning it as the broken lines. Curve round to form a circle, and glue the overlap. Snip felt overlapping the top edge to form tiny tabs, as indicated on the pattern. Turn the overlapping felt around the lower edge up inside the circle and glue to the card.

4. Rest the covered circle on the table, tabs upwards. With the felt side down, fit the lower half of the top over the circle, bringing the tabs up through the hole; glue the tabs neatly down over the card, so that the two pieces are firmly joined and the top sits level on the circle.

5. Felt side up, glue the upper part of the top over the under-side, keeping edges absolutely level. Blacken cut edges of card with a felt pen or drawing ink.

6. Make a small hole with a knitting needle or thin skewer in the centre top of the mortar board (see circle on the pattern).

7. Fold the ribbon in half and loop it around the knitting needle or thin skewer: twist the ribbon as much as you can, keeping it absolutely taut, then thread the twisted ribbon through the top of the tassel before folding it back on itself to form a twisted cord. Push the two ends through the hole in the top of the mortar board and knot them securely on the inside.

MISTRESS BARNOWL'S APRON AND CAP

MATERIALS
17 x 20cm (6½ x 8in) printed cotton-type fabric: lilac and pink flowers on black ground
Two 7cm (2¾in) diameter circles of lilac spotted voile (dotted Swiss)
60cm (¾yd) black lace, 10mm (⅜in) deep, for apron
70cm (¾yd) black lace, 10mm (⅜in) deep, for cap
Matching threads

1. Cut the apron and the waistband once each in printed fabric.

2. Turn under a very narrow hem around the sides and lower edge. Stitch lace flat on top, gathering neatly to turn the corners.

3. Gather the top edge and draw up to measure 10cm (4in). Right sides together and raw edges level, stitch one long edge of the waistband over the gathers, allowing the band to overlap equally at each end. Turn under the two short edges and tack. Fold the waistband in half lengthways, as broken line on pattern, turn under the other long raw edge and slip-stitch it over the gathers on the wrong side of the apron. Oversew each end. (continued on page 26)

HOLLOW · OAK
· HIGH SCHOOL ·

cat

4. Turn the waistband under and stitch to Mistress Barnowl's front at waist level, as illustrated.

5. Right sides together, join the two circles for the cap, leaving open between the notches. Trim the seam closely with pinking shears, then turn to the right side; fold in the raw edges and close remainder of seam. Top-stitch all round close to the edge.

6. Mark the edge of the circle equally into eight, with pins. Gather 40cm (16in) lace; mark this into eight also, then pin around the edge of the circle, matching marked points. Draw up the gathers to fit, distributing them evenly between the pins, and stitch into place.

7. Fold a 30cm (12in) length of lace in half and stitch the fold under the centre of the back edge of the cap, for streamers.

8. Stitch to Mistress Barnowl's head.

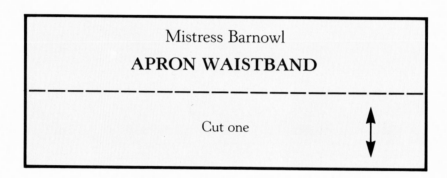

Mistress Barnowl

APRON WAISTBAND

Cut one

MISTRESS BARNOWL

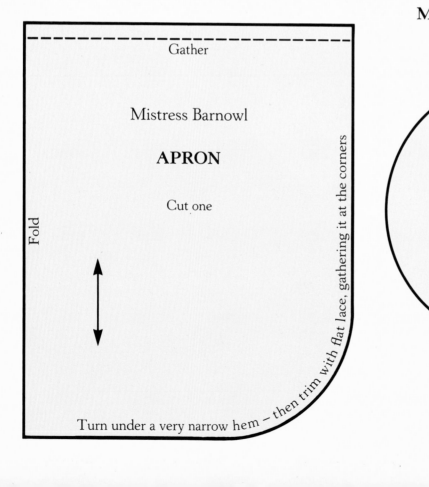

Gather

Mistress Barnowl

APRON

Cut one

Fold

Turn under a very narrow hem – then trim with flat lace, gathering it at the corners

Mistress Barnowl

CAP

Cut two

Leave open

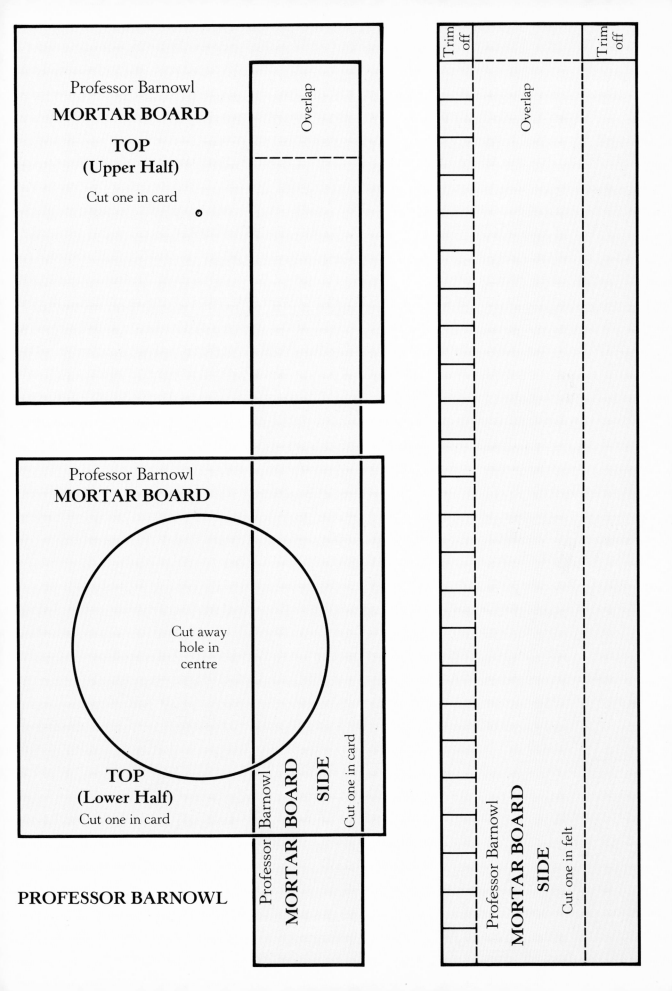

Professor Barnowl
MORTAR BOARD

TOP
(Upper Half)

Cut one in card

Overlap

Professor Barnowl
MORTAR BOARD

Cut away
hole in
centre

TOP
(Lower Half)

Cut one in card

Professor Barnowl
MORTAR BOARD
SIDE

Cut one in card

PROFESSOR BARNOWL

Professor Barnowl
MORTAR BOARD
SIDE

Cut one in card

Trim
off

Overlap

Trim
off

Professor Barnowl
MORTAR BOARD
SIDE

Cut one in felt

The Harvest Mice go on Holiday

Stationmaster Speedwell didn't know which way to turn. The ticket clerk had gone to the dentist, the porter was in bed with a cold and the signalman was visiting his auntie in hospital. To make matters worse, today the harvest mice were going on holiday.

'I just can't manage on my own,' he grumbled, 'I need help.' Then he remembered the poster he had seen the day before, and sighed with relief. 'I'll call in the pixies!' he decided.

Flip and Flop nearly forgot to put their hats on in their hurry to get to Blackberry Halt.

'Do you think we'll drive the train?' Flop asked excitedly.

'No, of course not. We're station staff,' replied Flip grandly.

Stationmaster Speedwell gave them their orders. 'Flip, you sit in the ticket office,' he said. 'Tickets cost two nuts for adults; children half-price. And Flop, sweep the platform, pick up those parcels, water the window boxes, and generally make yourself useful.'

Flip had only just settled himself behind the little window of the ticket office when Harvey Mouse arrived with his wife and eight children.

'Two adults. That's four nuts. And eight more half-price. That's twelve nuts altogether please,' said Flip proudly.

Harvey Mouse counted out the nuts. Flip checked them and put them into a sack on the floor. Then Flop carried their luggage onto the platform. The young mice behaved very badly and chased each other all over the station. Their parents smiled tolerantly, and the children took no notice when Flip and Flop tried to stop them. Stationmaster Speedwell kept glancing at his watch as he waited for the train to come and take the mice to the seaside.

'Here you are,' he said, handing Flip and Flop two flags, 'the red one is for stop and the green one means go.'

Flip and Flop felt very important as they signalled the train to stop for the mice and then waved it off again.

'Thank you for a good day's work,' smiled the stationmaster as the train disappeared round Blackberry Hill, leaving a trail of white smoke. 'Here's your pay.'

Back home in Toadstool Cottage Flip and Flop stared at the bag of nuts.

'What are we going to do with those?' Flop said.

'Eat them, of course,' replied Flip.

'But what about our television set?' moaned Flop.

'Nuts to that,' sighed Flip, and set to work making two tasty nut cutlets for their supper.

STATIONMASTER SPEEDWELL

With his penchant for fast travel and his ability to plan ahead, the squirrel makes an ideal stationmaster. He can be relied upon to know whether the trains are running on time, to check that the signals are working properly, to have plenty of tickets in the booking office, and to make sure there is no litter making his station untidy. (But don't look too closely under the platform — that's where he hoards his nuts!)

Acorn Speedwell isn't too keen on the harvest mice running wild all over his station. But he understands they are over-excited because they are going on holiday. Nevertheless, he can't help feeling that if Mr and Mrs Harvey Mouse insist on having such a large family, they really should attempt to keep them in order.

This amusing little character makes a wonderful mascot for railway enthusiasts of any age: but if he is for a small child, omit buttons, beads and watch-chain.

First turn to page 105 to make the basic Adult Squirrel; then continue below.

MATERIALS
30cm (12in) navy blue felt, 90cm (36in) wide
7 x 18cm (2¾ x 7in) black felt
30cm (12in) black single-face satin ribbon, 12mm (½in) wide, for cap
4.25m (4¾yd) gold metallic grosgrain ribbon, 1.5mm (1/16in) wide (to make gold braid)
50cm (½yd) black braid, about 10mm (⅜in) wide, to fold round edge of peak, etc.
1 large ornamental gilt button, about 2.5cm (1in) diameter, for cap
6 tiny gilt buttons, about 10mm (⅜in) diameter
6 small gilt beads, about 3-4mm (⅛in) diameter
10cm (4in) medium-weight chain (silver or gilt), for watch-chain
20 x 30cm (8 x 12in) thin card
9 x 7cm (3½ x 2¾in) medium card
Matching threads
Dry-stick adhesive (optional)
Clear adhesive

(*Note:* before actually cutting out the pieces as directed in step 1, check to ensure that you will have a suitable area of felt left to cut the top and side of the cap as directed in steps 11 and 14.)

1. Cut the trousers, and the coat front, back and sleeve, and the waistcoat (vest), twice each (reverse the front, back and waistcoat patterns), all in blue felt: cut the collar once. Open out both trouser pieces and cut away the tail section at one corner only (reverse the second piece).

2. Oversew each trouser piece together between a-b. Then join the two pieces together between c-a-d, to form the centre front and back seams. Turn to the right side.

3. Gather the top edge (between e-e), then fit trousers on squirrel and draw up round the waist, catching the back corners (e-e) securely together with a thread taken from side to side through the tail several times (use a darning needle to do this).

4. Overlap the front edges of the waistcoat as indicated by the broken line, and tack together. Stitch beads down centre front, through the double felt, at (o)s. Remove the tacking thread.
    Stitch the ends of the watch-chain at (x)s, so that it hangs as illustrated.

5. Place waistcoat flat on his chest, taking the side edges (f-f) round and pinning them to the back of the body, and over the trousers. Take the top points of the waistcoat (g) over the shoulders and round the neck, pinning to the body just behind the head. Make sure the waistcoat fits smoothly, then stitch the top pieces and sides to the body and trousers, removing the pins.

6. To make the coat, oversew the front pieces to the back at each shoulder (h-j).
    Gather the top edge of each sleeve between the circles. Fit the sleeves into the armholes, matching the side edges (k) and centre top to the shoulder seam (j). Draw up the gathers to fit and stitch into place.
    Join the sleeve and side seams (l-k-m). Join the two pieces together down the centre back seam (n-p).

7. With the right side of the collar to the inside of the coat, stitch the collar round the neck edge between h-
(continued on page 34)

STATIONMASTER SPEEDWELL

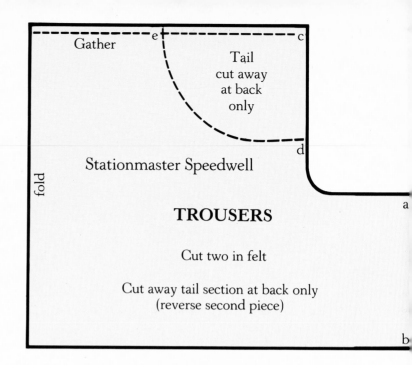

Gather

e   c

Tail
cut away
at back
only

d

fold

Stationmaster Speedwell

a

TROUSERS

Cut two in felt

Cut away tail section at back only
(reverse second piece)

b

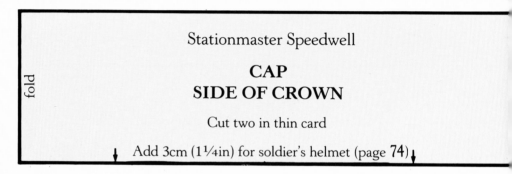

fold

Stationmaster Speedwell

CAP
SIDE OF CROWN

Cut two in thin card

↓ Add 3cm (1¼in) for soldier's helmet (page 74) ↓

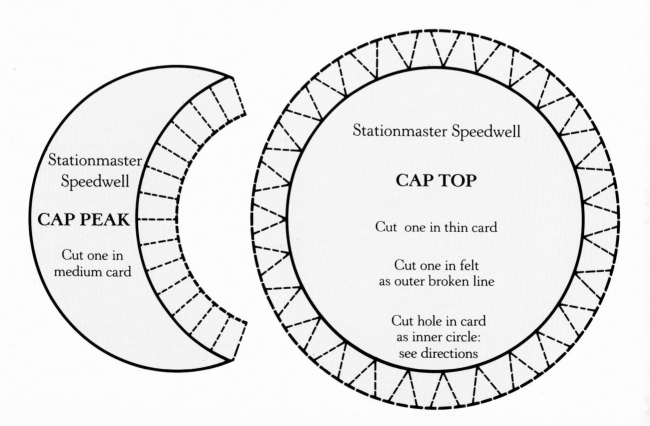

Stationmaster
Speedwell

CAP PEAK

Cut one in
medium card

Stationmaster Speedwell

CAP TOP

Cut one in thin card

Cut one in felt
as outer broken line

Cut hole in card
as inner circle:
see directions

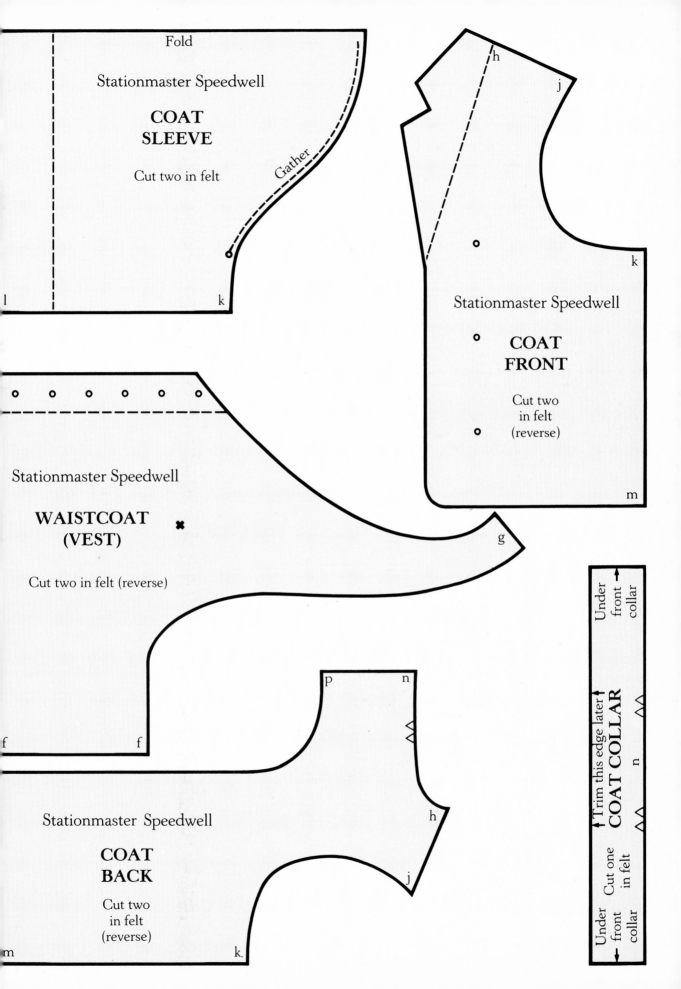

Fold

Stationmaster Speedwell

**COAT
SLEEVE**

Cut two in felt

Gather

l   k

h

j

k

Stationmaster Speedwell

**COAT
FRONT**

Cut two
in felt
(reverse)

m

Stationmaster Speedwell

**WAISTCOAT
(VEST)**

✖

Cut two in felt (reverse)

g

p   n

f   f

h

Stationmaster Speedwell

**COAT
BACK**

Cut two
in felt
(reverse)

m   k

j

Under front collar

← Trim this edge later

COAT COLLAR

Cut one
in felt

n

Under front collar

h, matching centres (n) and double notches (the collar should overlap slightly at each end). Then turn the coat to the right side, turning the collar over to the outside, and glue each end of the back collar *under* the front collar (making sure that the back edge of the front collar forms a right-angle with the seam you have just made). Finally, trim the outer edge of the back collar level with the front collar.

8. Plait three 25cm (10in) lengths of gold ribbon to make braid (see Trimmings: page 8): stitch or glue carefully round the edge of the collar, beginning and ending at the top corner of each lapel.

Stitch or glue the collar down to hold in position.

Make two similar lengths of braid and glue them round the sleeves as broken line on the pattern.

9. Stitch three buttons to each coat front, at (o)s.

10. Fit the coat on the squirrel and, if necessary, catch the lower corners together at the back by stitching through the tail, as for the trousers.

11. To make the cap, cut the top once and the side twice, in thin card. Cut the peak once in medium card (ignore broken lines). Cut a larger circle in felt for the top, following the outer broken line.

12. Cut a hole exactly the same size as the card top in any piece of spare card. Roll up one side strip of card, fit it inside the hole and allow it to open out so that it fits snugly; mark the overlap, then remove and glue to form a cylinder.

13. Glue the card circle in the centre of the felt for the top (use a glue-stick, if you have one, to stick card to felt); then snip out V-shapes all the way round, as indicated, to form tiny tabs.

Place the top, felt side down, on a flat surface; place the side cylinder upside-down on top, and carefully bring the tabs up and glue them all round the top edge.

14. Wrap the second card strip round the side cylinder and trim off the excess, so that it fits exactly. Glue the strip to felt, then trim the felt level with one short and both long edges; leave a 1cm (3/8in) overlap at the remaining edge. Glue this strip neatly round over the first strip, top and bottom edges level and join at the back.

15. Cover the top of the peak with black felt and trim the felt level with the card all round. Cover the underside in the same way, but trim only the outer edge level; allow a surplus along the inner edge as indicated by the broken lines. Snip this surplus into tiny tabs, as shown, then carefully glue these up inside the front of the cap to hold the peak in position (make sure you have the inner edge of the peak fitting snugly against the bottom edge of the cap).

16. Glue black braid round the outer edge of the peak, folding it over the edge. Glue a band of black braid around the top edge of the cap. Then make a length of plaited gold braid from three 40cm (16in) lengths of metallic ribbon, and glue round the lower edge. Glue a band of black satin ribbon immediately above the gold braid. Plait another piece of gold braid, from three 25cm (10in) lengths of ribbon, and glue round the peak, inside, and close against, the black braid edge.

Finally, fix the large button to the centre front of the cap.

MR AND MRS HARVEY MOUSE
AND FAMILY

Large or small, the harvest mice have lots of sales appeal. A slick, streamlined design which is ideal for mass-production — whilst still retaining a high degree of individuality.

With a combination of imagination and ingenuity you can use the adult mouse pattern as a basis for any number of amusing characters. Hunt through your box of bits and pieces for inspiration, or look at the pocket-money section in your local toyshop. One small accessory will suggest a character, and once you get started, the ideas will come thick and fast. Then you will be able to offer your customers an eye-catching collection from which to choose their own special mascot.

Children (and car-owners) will love the baby mouse. Look for a rich golden-brown felt the colour of sun-ripened corn for either size mouse: but dress the babies in clear, brightly contrasting colours. Decide whether it's to be a baby girl in a lace-trimmed dress or a boy in a T-shirt and trousers or workmouselike dungarees. Then select the appropriate materials from the list below.

The basic pattern looks almost too simple. But the secret is in the stuffing — a very well-filled shape — followed by a crafty gathering thread to rescue the waistline. Your stitches will show slightly, so try to make them as small and close together as possible — and match your thread carefully too.

BABY MOUSE

MATERIALS

15cm (6in) square golden-brown felt for boy in T-shirt
   or girl
or 18cm (7in) square golden-brown felt for boy in dungarees
Scrap of black felt
4 x 17cm (1⅝ x 6¾in) felt for trousers or pantalettes
   (white)
4 x 20cm (1⅝ x 8in) felt for dungarees
5 x 9cm (2 x 3½in) felt for dress bodice or T-shirt
4 x 20cm (1½ x 8in) fabric for skirt
Lace, ribbons and flowers to trim: see individual directions
   in steps 15, 16, 17 and 21
Polyester stuffing
15cm (6in) golden-brown lacing cord for tail

2.5cm (1in) diameter circle of stiff card (cereal carton)
Matching threads
Clear adhesive

1. For a mouse wearing dungarees, cut the head gusset and the body once each in brown felt, the face, ear and foot twice each, and the arm four times (reverse two). Cut the base circle in card. If you are making a boy in a T-shirt or a girl, omit the body.

For a boy in dungarees, cut the trousers and the bib once each in contrast felt, and the strap twice.

For a mouse wearing T-shirt and trousers, cut the body and trousers once each in contrasting felts.

For a baby girl, cut the pantalettes in white felt. Cut the body in a felt to match or tone with skirt fabric.

2. Oversew the two face pieces together between A-B. Carefully match the tip of the gusset (A) to the top of the seam; then join it to each side of the face between A-C. It is important to do this very accurately and neatly, as these seams determine the shape of the face and head. Turn to the right side.

3. Stuff the head very firmly, pushing the filling well up into the nose and chin. Using a double thread, gather round the lower edge of the head, then draw up tightly and secure (before securing your thread, check that the head is sufficiently stuffed, adding a little more filling under the chin and at the back of the head). Make sure the head is a good shape — partly by moulding it with your fingers, and also by moving the filling around inside with a strong darning needle pushed through the base.

4. Mark the notches on the lower edge of the body and the top edge of the trousers/pantalettes. Gather the top edge of the trousers/pantalettes as indicated, then (right sides together) pin to the lower edge of the body, matching side edges and notches. Draw up to fit and oversew together. Join the centre back seam of the trousers/pantalettes, then gather the lower edge (with a double thread); draw up tightly and secure.

5. Glue the card base circle centrally over the little gathered base hole at the bottom of the body, then

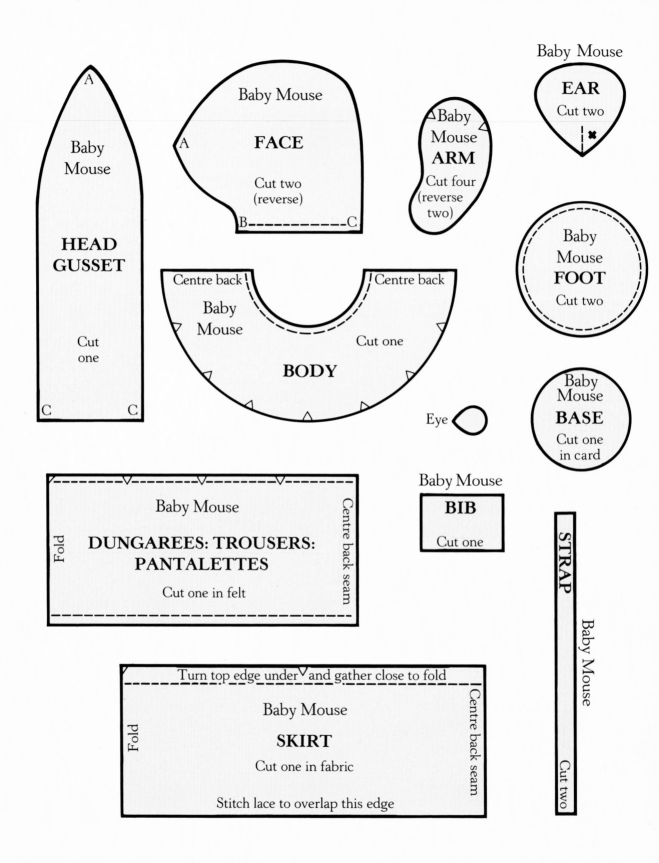

A

Baby
Mouse

HEAD
GUSSET

Cut
one

C   C

Baby Mouse

FACE

A

Cut two
(reverse)

B ----------- C

Baby
Mouse
ARM

Cut four
(reverse
two)

Baby Mouse

EAR

Cut two

✖

Baby
Mouse
FOOT

Cut two

Baby
Mouse
BASE

Cut one
in card

Centre back   Centre back

Baby
Mouse

Cut one

BODY

Eye

Baby Mouse

BIB

Cut one

Fold

Baby Mouse

DUNGAREES: TROUSERS:
PANTALETTES

Cut one in felt

Centre back seam

STRAP

Baby Mouse

Cut two

Fold

Turn top edge under and gather close to fold

Baby Mouse

SKIRT

Cut one in fabric

Stitch lace to overlap this edge

Centre back seam

BABY MOUSE

carefully turn to the right side. Join the centre back seam of the body; it should be possible to do this on the inside, working from the outside — but if you find this fiddly, just make a neatly oversewn seam on the right side.

6. Stuff the body very thoroughly, working the filling down into the lower part so that the trousers/pantalettes are completely filled; then stuff the upper part of the body before gathering round the top edge with a double thread. Insert a bit more stuffing before drawing up your gathers tightly and securing the thread.

7. Using a double thread, take a stitch underneath the gathered circle at the top of the body, from back to front. Then take a stitch under the gathered circle at the base of the head, from front to back and repeat the first stitch through the body. Draw up to fix the head in position, and take three more stitches to hold it firmly in place. Now ladder stitch all round, alternately taking one stitch through the head and one through the body, securing them firmly together; when the head is correctly positioned, go round again, drawing your thread tighter.

8. Beginning and ending at the centre back seam, and using a double thread, gather round the top edge of the trousers/pantalettes, close against the seam. Then draw up to shape the body as illustrated, and secure.

9. For the BABY's arm, pin two pieces *wrong sides facing,* and oversew together all round, leaving the top open between the notches. Stuff firmly, pushing well down into the paw, then complete oversewing round the top.

For the ADULT arm, join a paw to the bottom of each sleeve piece. Then pin two sleeve/paw pieces *right sides facing,* and oversew together all round, leaving the top open between the notches. Turn to the right side. Stuff firmly, pushing well down into the paw, then oversew the top edges together.

10. Stitch the top of each arm to the side of the body, close under the head.

11. For each foot, gather close to the edge of the circle. Then place a small ball of stuffing in the centre and draw up tightly, but don't stitch together in a circle; instead, oversew the gathered edges together, side-by-side, to make an oval-shaped foot (figures 1 and 2).

12. Pin the feet under the front of the body to determine their position (figure 3), then stitch securely.

13. To achieve the correct shape and balance of the body, push the mouse's tummy in and draw the behind back (study the photograph for guidance); to do this, place your forefinger over the top of the centre back seam of the trousers — and your thumb underneath the body, over the gathered centre of the base: then pinch hard, drawing the base back as far as you can with your thumbnail.

14. Smear the cut ends of the lacing cord with a tiny blob of adhesive and roll between your fingertips to seal and form a point at each end. Select one end for the tip of the tail, and make a knot close to the other end. Stitch the knot over the centre back seam, close to the gathered base (X on figure 3), so that it balances the body and enables the mouse to stand firmly.

15. For the dungarees, join the lower edge of the bib to the top edge of the trousers, right sides together, and centre fronts matching. Bring the bib up and glue the end of a strap under each top corner. Take the straps smoothly over the shoulders, cross at the back, and glue to the waist edge of the trousers, trimming off the excess.

Glue on a scrap of embroidery or lace to trim the bib.

16. For a mouse wearing trousers and T-shirt, add braces made either from strips of felt using the strap pattern, or from 3mm (1/8in) wide grosgrain ribbon. Stitch the front ends of the straps at waist level, about 15-20mm (1/2-3/4in) apart; cross over at the back and finish the ends at the waist.

17. For a baby girl, join the side edges of the skirt to form the centre back seam. Turn to the right side. Trim the hem with 10mm (3/8in) deep lace, sewing it to overlap the raw lower edge. Turn the top edge over and gather very close to the fold. Mark the notches, then fit on the mouse, pinning the marked points

Figure 1: 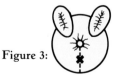   **Figure 2:**

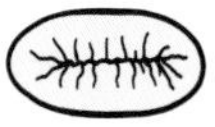

BASE OF FOOT   **SIDE OF FOOT**

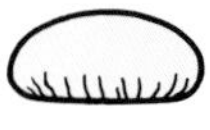

Figure 3:

BASE OF MOUSE:
Approximate position of feet

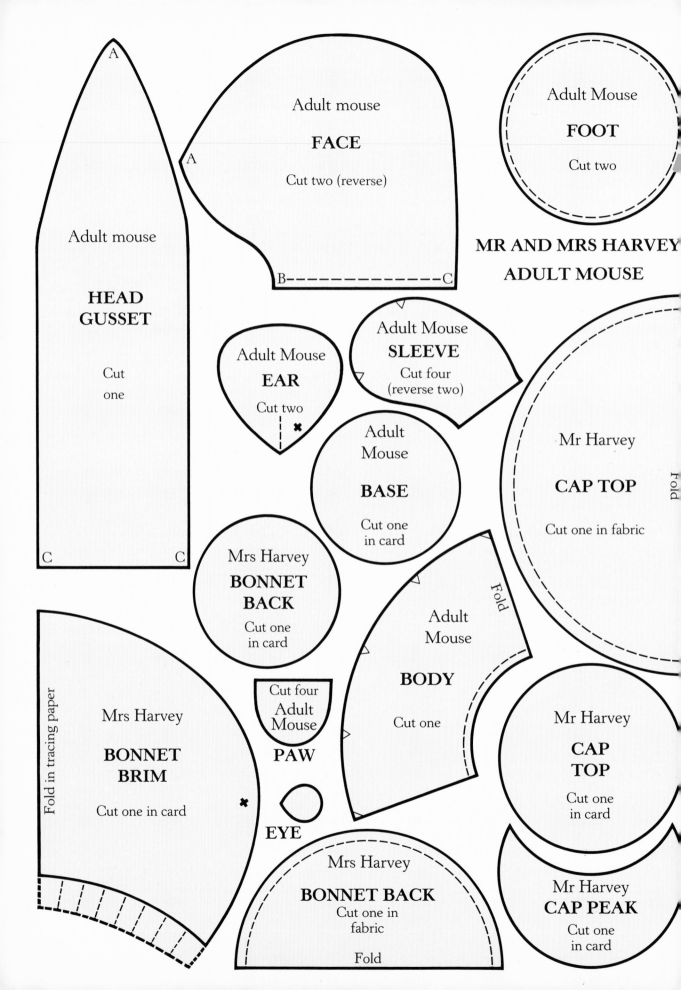

A

Adult mouse

HEAD GUSSET

Cut one

C   C

Adult mouse

FACE

Cut two (reverse)

A

B – – – – – – – – – – – C

Adult Mouse **FOOT**

Cut two

MR AND MRS HARVEY

ADULT MOUSE

Adult Mouse **EAR**

Cut two

Adult Mouse **SLEEVE**

Cut four (reverse two)

Adult Mouse **BASE**

Cut one in card

Mr Harvey **CAP TOP**

Cut one in fabric

Fold

Mrs Harvey **BONNET BACK**

Cut one in card

Adult Mouse **BODY**

Cut one

Fold

Mr Harvey **CAP TOP**

Cut one in card

Fold in tracing paper

Mrs Harvey **BONNET BRIM**

Cut one in card

Cut four Adult Mouse **PAW**

EYE

Mrs Harvey **BONNET BACK**

Cut one in fabric

Fold

Mr Harvey **CAP PEAK**

Cut one in card

at side and centre front. Draw up the gathers, distributing them evenly round the waist, and catch into position.

Add a lace collar, made from 15cm (6in) lace, gathered and drawn up around the neck. Or have lace straps over the shoulders, stitching the centre of the lace at the centre front of the waist and joining the two ends at the centre back; you will need 15cm (6in) lace for flat straps, or 25cm (10in) if they are gathered.

For a party frock, add a butterfly bow (see Trimmings: page 8) at the back, made from 15cm (6in) 9mm (3/8in) wide single-face satin ribbon: points B 3.5cm (1 3/8in) from A.

18. Put a spot of adhesive inside each ear at X, then fold as the broken line and pinch together. Pin to the sides of the head.

19. Cut the eyes in black felt and pin to the sides of the head.

20. Check the position of the eyes and ears in relation to each other, moving them around until you are satisfied. Then glue into place.

21. Trim the girls' heads with tiny flowers sewn between the ears or with 20cm (8in) lace tightly gathered into a circle and sewn to the top of the head with a lace daisy in the centre; or with a butterfly bow, either made from 20cm (8in) feather-edge (cream in photograph) satin ribbon, 5mm (1/4in) wide (points B 3cm (1 1/4in) from A), or made from 15cm (6in) double-face (red in photograph) satin ribbon, 9mm (3/8in) wide (points B 4.5cm (1 3/4in) from A).

ADULT MOUSE

MATERIALS
23cm (9in) square golden-brown felt
Scrap of black felt
15cm (6in) square contrast felt for body and sleeves
6 x 25cm (2 3/8 x 10in) white felt for pantalettes (mother)
10 x 65cm (4 x 26in) fabric for skirt and bonnet (mother)
11 x 40cm (4 1/4 x 15in) fabric (or felt) for trousers and cap (father)
10 x 15cm (4 x 6in) toning felt for cap (father)
12.5cm (5in) square lightweight fabric for scarf (father)
20cm (8in) grosgrain ribbon, 3mm (1/8in) wide, for braces (father)
20cm (8in) feather-edge satin ribbon, 5mm (1/4in) wide (mother)
1.8m (2yd) lace, 10mm (3/8in) deep (mother)
Polyester stuffing
20cm (8in) golden-brown lacing cord for tail
10 x 20cm (4 x 8in) thin plain white card for bonnet (mother)
6 x 12cm (2 1/2 x 5in) stiff card (cereal carton) for cap (father)
4cm (1 5/8in) diameter circle of stiff card (cereal carton) for base
Matching threads
Dry-stick adhesive (mother)
Clear adhesive

1. Cut the head gusset once, the face, ear and foot twice each, and the paw four times, in brown felt. Glue the two ears to more felt and cut round level with the edge, to make them double thickness. Cut the body once and the sleeve four times (reverse two) in contrast felt. Cut mother's pantalettes in white felt. If using fabric for father's trousers, allow an extra 6-7mm (1/4in) all round: turn this edge under and tack, then treat as felt (but if actually using felt, cut as mother's pantalettes).

Cut the base circle in stiff card.

2. Follow the directions for the Baby Mouse, steps 2-14 inclusive noting the alternative directions for the arm in step 9: then add the features as steps 18, 19 and 20.

3. Make and fit mother's skirt as the baby girl, step 17. Stitch or glue a lace cuff around each wrist. Gather 40cm (16in) lace; catch the centre at the centre front of the waist, then take the ends up and join at back of neck, drawing up the gathers and distributing them evenly.

4. Cut mother's bonnet brim in thin card, ignoring the broken lines. Using the glue-stick, cover one side (the outside) with fabric; trim level with the outer edge, but leave a surplus around the inner curve as the broken lines, and snip into tabs as indicated; fold them over the edge of the card and stick to the under-side of the brim. Cover the under-side with fabric in the same way, but trim it level all round. Cut the large back in fabric and gather all around the edge. Cut the small back in card and place it in the centre of the fabric circle (on wrong side of fabric); draw up the gathers tightly and secure. Oversew the back edge of the brim around the bonnet back.

5. Gather about 60cm (24in) lace and glue it evenly *all around* the brim, overlapping the edge as illustrated. Gather another 10cm (4in) and glue it *inside* the lower edge of the back — so that the back circle is entirely surrounded by lace.

6. Stitch one end of a 10cm (4in) length of feather-edge ribbon inside the bonnet at X. Fit the bonnet on the mouse, taking the ribbon under her chin; using a long darning needle, fix the bonnet in position by stitching right through the head, between the Xs, slipping the other end of the ribbon inside the brim as you do so. Stitch through the head several times to hold the bonnet firmly in place. Finally, make a butterfly bow (see Trimmings: page 8) with the remaining ribbon (points B 3cm (1¼in) from A), and stitch or glue under the chin over the centre of the previous piece.

7. Stitch the centre of the grosgrain ribbon to the top of father's trousers at the centre back; bring the ends over his shoulders and stitch at the front, about 4cm (1½in) apart, trimming off the surplus and turning each raw end under.

8. Draw threads from the edge of the scarf fabric to form a fringe, then fold into a triangle and knot around father's neck.

9. To make his cap, cut circles of felt, fabric and card as patterns. Gather all round the edge of the felt circle, place the card one inside, draw up the gathers and secure the thread. Gather the fabric circle in the same way, then place the previous piece, smooth side down, in the centre on the wrong side of the fabric, then draw up the gathers and secure as before.

10. Cut the peak in stiff card and cover one side with felt, trimming it level all round: then cover the other side in the same way. Glue the peak under the cap, so that it protrudes just under 1cm (⅜in). Stitch or glue cap to the top of his head.

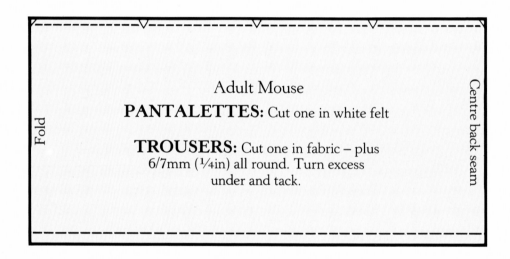

Adult Mouse

PANTALETTES: Cut one in white felt

TROUSERS: Cut one in fabric – plus 6/7mm (¼in) all round. Turn excess under and tack.

Fold

Centre back seam

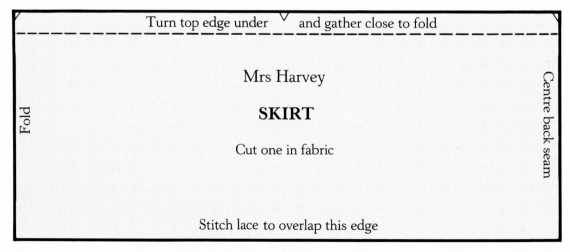

Turn top edge under and gather close to fold

Mrs Harvey

SKIRT

Cut one in fabric

Fold

Centre back seam

Stitch lace to overlap this edge

THE MOUSE FAMILY'S

 ## LUGGAGE

When you have eight children to pack for — *and a golfing husband* — you need plenty of luggage. Mrs Harvey Mouse just managed to squeeze everything into two suitcases, a bucket bag and her biggest shopping basket. Her husband's golf clubs are safely stowed in a smart bag, and he has an outsize umbrella in case rain threatens to stop play.

SUITCASE

MATERIALS
Two 7 x 10cm (2¾ x 4in) pieces of medium-weight
  cotton-type fabric
Stiff card (cereal carton)
40cm (½yd) satin ribbon, 1.5mm (1/16in) wide
or 4cm (1½in) narrow braid
Dry-stick adhesive (optional)
Clear adhesive

1. Cut a piece of card as diagram: score broken lines with a blunt knife.

2. Fold round to form a box and glue flap (a) *behind* side (a) (inside). Bend up tabs (b) and push inside, then fold tabs (c) and (d) round and stick one over the other.

3. Glue a 7 x 10cm (2¾ x 4in) piece of fabric over one side, overlapping equally all round, then cut the corners neatly and stick the surplus smoothly over the top, base and ends. Repeat for the other side.

4. Plait ribbon to make braid (Trimmings: page 8). Trim to measure 8.5cm (3¼in), then fold ends under to meet at centre, and glue. Curve over to form a handle and glue to top of suitcase.

BUCKET BAG

MATERIALS
12 x 20cm (5 x 8in) medium-weight cotton-type fabric
Stiff card (cereal carton)
20cm (¼yd) ribbon, 3mm (1/8in) wide
Clear adhesive

1. Cut fabric for sides of bag. Snip lower edge into small tabs as indicated.

2. Cut the base circle in card, then again, slightly smaller. Glue second circle to wrong side of remaining fabric; cut fabric as indicated on pattern, and snip the surplus into V-shaped notches; then turn tabs neatly over edge of card and glue to back. Set aside.

3. Curve the snipped lower edge of the fabric round the larger card base and glue tabs underneath. Glue join where the fabric overlaps. Glue the covered card circle neatly underneath.

4. Fold upper part of fabric down inside bag and glue lightly (adjust depth to suit yourself).

5. Cut two 10cm (4½in) lengths of ribbon; glue ends neatly inside bag to form a handle at each side.

SHOPPING BASKET

MATERIALS
Natural garden raffia

1. Place two strands of raffia together and tie a knot at one end. Holding the cut end underneath, wrap the section of raffia next to the knot smoothly round it, stitching to the knot with a thin strand of raffia.

MAKING STRAW HATS
AND BASKETS

2. Continue round and round, until you have a flat circle about 3.5-4cm (1⅜-1½in) in diameter; then gently curve the shape upwards, by stitching the raffia at a slight angle to the previous round.

3. Work upwards to form the sides of the basket, curving in slightly as illustrated. When the basket is 2.5cm (1in) deep, curve outwards to form a rim, then cut the raffia and finish neatly inside.

4. To make the handle, place eight 10cm (4in) lengths of raffia together and bind tightly and neatly with another strand of raffia. Trim the ends, then curve over top of basket and stitch at each side.

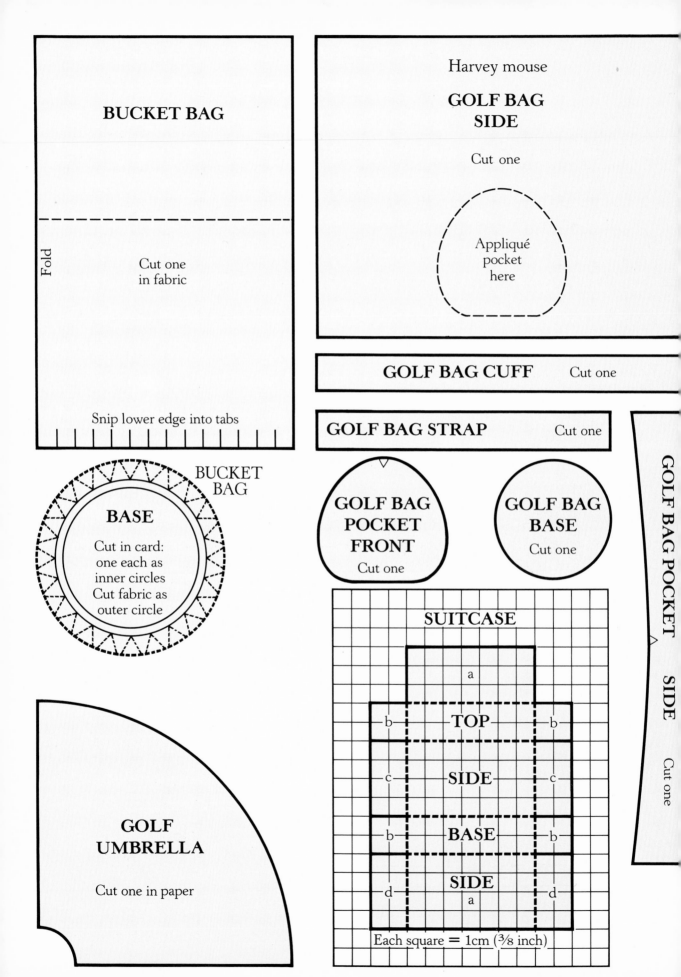

BUCKET BAG

Fold

Cut one
in fabric

Snip lower edge into tabs

**BUCKET
BAG**

BASE

Cut in card:
one each as
inner circles
Cut fabric as
outer circle

**GOLF
UMBRELLA**

Cut one in paper

Harvey mouse

**GOLF BAG
SIDE**

Cut one

Appliqué
pocket
here

GOLF BAG CUFF   Cut one

GOLF BAG STRAP   Cut one

**GOLF BAG
POCKET
FRONT**

Cut one

**GOLF BAG
BASE**

Cut one

GOLF BAG POCKET   SIDE

Cut one

SUITCASE

a

b   **TOP**   b

c   **SIDE**   c

b   **BASE**   b

   SIDE

d   a   d

Each square = 1cm (⅜ inch)

GOLF BAG

MATERIALS
15cm (6in) square felt
Cotton wool (absorbent cotton) or stuffing
Small cylindrical container (about 4cm (1½in) high x
    2cm (¾in) diameter)
    or greaseproof paper
Modelling clay
Clear adhesive

1. Cut each piece once in felt.

2. With the *wrong sides together* and matching the notches, oversew one long edge of the pocket side round the pocket front; join the short ends of the side where they overlap.

3. Pin to bag as indicated on pattern and appliqué into place; push in a little stuffing just before you finish.

4. With wrong sides together, oversew lower edge of bag round edge of base. Overlap side edges and slip-stitch join.

5. Glue cuff round the top edge.

6. Stitch one end of strap to top edge of pocket front, then glue other end just inside top of bag.

7. Fill container with modelling clay (or wrap) and place inside to add weight.

GOLF CLUBS

MATERIALS
Corn stalks or very thin sticks
Modelling clay (self-hardening or plastic)
Coloured paints if necessary
Clear adhesive

1. Model the heads of the clubs as illustrated and allow to dry, if necessary.

2. Paint, if necessary, then glue on corn stalk handles.

GOLF UMBRELLA

MATERIALS
13cm (5in) plastic-covered wire
Medium-weight white paper
25cm (10in) single-face satin ribbon, 9mm (⅜in) wide in
    each of *three* colours
Matching thread
Cotton wool (absorbent cotton) or stuffing
Dry-stick adhesive
Clear adhesive

1. Straighten out the wire, then bend as figure 1 to form handle.

2. Cut paper as pattern (and figure 2). Using the glue-stick fix a strip of ribbon level with one straight edge (figure 3); trim level with top edge of paper, but overlap the lower edge 1cm (⅜in). Stick a contrasting strip of ribbon next to, and over, the first, positioning it as figure 4. Repeat with another contrasting strip of ribbon as figure 5.

3. Repeat twice more — making nine strips of ribbon. Trim the lower corner so the ribbon overlaps the edge of the paper just a fraction, then curve round to form a cone and glue join, overlapping ribbon to conform.

4. Slip the wire through the centre and fix with cotton wool glued inside.

5. Fold the top edge between the strips of ribbon to form pleats: stitch through each, then draw up thread and secure.

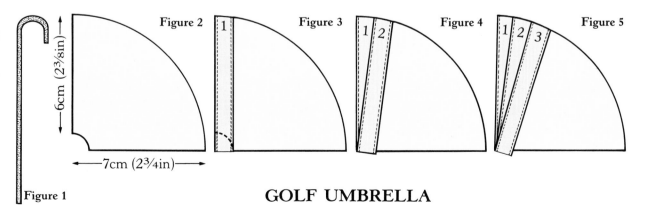

Figure 1   Figure 2   Figure 3   Figure 4   Figure 5

6cm (2⅜in)   7cm (2¾in)

GOLF UMBRELLA

43

Silvery Grey Weds Barleycorn Brown

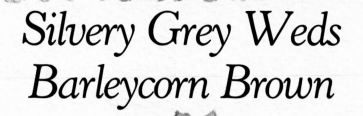

Flip looked out of the kitchen window. Flop was talking to a plump grey rabbit. He guessed they were discussing her daughter's wedding to Barleycorn Brown. Mrs Grey had talked of nothing else for weeks.

Flop came running in. 'Mrs Grey wants us to supply rose petal confetti for Silvery's wedding,' he panted. Then he frowned: 'What's confetti?'

'Stuff you throw over the bride and bridegroom,' Flip answered.

'Mrs Grey's having a great big hat covered in pink roses,' Flop continued, 'she says Madame Florette's making it and it will be a sensation.'

Millie Haystack was a fieldmouse who had once crossed the Blackberry Stream on a day-trip to Paris. On her return she had adopted the name Madame Florette and set up in business as a fashionable milliner.

While Madame Florette cut out hundreds of delicate pink silk petals and fashioned them into enormous full-blown roses, Flip and Flop searched the Hollow for wild roses and filled a sack with the petals.

Silvery looked beautiful on her wedding day. And her little nieces, Violet and Primrose, looked sweet with forget-me-nots between their ears. Barleycorn's small nephew was dressed as a smart young midshipman.

Mrs Grey put on her new hat. Madame Florette had succeeded; the hat was a sensation. But when she reached the church Mrs Grey had a headache, so she took the hat off until the wedding ceremony began.

Flip and Flop arrived at the church with their sack. But when they emptied it, the rose petals were all stuck together in a horrid soggy mess.

'Quick,' whispered Flip in a panic, 'we'll have to find some more.'

They looked all round the churchyard, but there were only buttercups and daisies growing in the grass. Then, peeping through the door, Flop spotted a mass of pink rose petals.

Flip sighed with relief as they hurried back with their sack full of fresh pink petals: 'Well done!' Flop grinned proudly.

Inside the church Mrs Grey was having hysterics. 'Where's my hat?' she demanded. 'I put it down here.'

'Is this it?' asked the vicar, picking up a straw shape trimmed with a few straggly green leaves.

'No . . . YES!' screeched Mrs Grey. 'What has happened to all the roses?' No-one could tell her.

But afterwards, as the guests laughingly threw confetti over the happy couple, Mrs Grey looked at the delicate silk petals scattered on the grass . . . and she knew exactly what had happened to the roses on her hat.

Which is why Flip and Flop didn't get paid for that job either.

THE MIDSHIPMAN
PAGE

His smart straw boater is charming, but if you're short of time, he still has considerable appeal without it. The little sailor top is very quick and easy.

MATERIALS

20cm (8in) camel-colour fur fabric, 70cm (27in) wide
Cream fur fabric, 7cm (3in) deep x 10cm (4in) wide
5 x 10cm (2 x 4in) camel felt (to tone with fur)
3cm (1¼in) square black felt
White pompon, 3cm (1¼in) diameter
  or fluffy white knitting yarn, for tail
Polyester stuffing
Matching threads
Scraps of stiff card or plastic (double cereal carton or
  cottage cheese lid)
Clear adhesive

25cm (10in) square deep blue felt
70cm (¾yd) narrow white piping cord
Natural garden raffia for hat
15cm (6in) single-face black satin ribbon, 9mm (⅜in)
  wide, for tunic
30cm (12in) single-face black satin ribbon, 9mm (⅜in)
  wide, for hat
20cm (8in) narrow round black elastic for hat
Matching threads
Clear adhesive (as above)

1. Use the pattern pieces for the Junior Rabbit (page 104). In camel fur fabric, cut the head gusset and body once, the face and leg twice each, and the arm (reverse two) and ear four times. Cut the body once more in cream fur (for his chest). Cut the sole twice in felt: then cut it again slightly smaller, following the broken line, in card or stiff plastic. Mark notches.

2. Turn to page 100 and follow the directions for the 'all-fur' version of the basic Adult Rabbit (omit the mouth).

3. In blue felt, cut the tunic back and collar once, and the front and sleeve twice each.

4. Oversew the front pieces to the back at the shoulders. Gather the top edge of each sleeve between the circles, then set into the armholes, matching side edges, notches and centre top of sleeve to the shoulder seam; draw up the gathers to fit and stitch into place. Join the side and sleeve seams.

5. With the right side of the collar to the wrong side of the tunic, pin together round the neck edge, matching notches; have the front points of the collar level with the broken lines on the tunic fronts. Stitch neatly into place, then turn the collar over to the outside.

6. Either stitch or glue piping cord around the collar and cuffs, as indicated by broken lines. Finish cut ends neatly, binding tightly with thread.

7. Fold centre front edges under along broken line and glue lightly to hold. Fit tunic on rabbit, then slip-stitch folded centre front edges together. Catch the front corners of the collar down to hold in position.

8. Make a butterfly bow (see Trimmings: page 8) from 12.5cm (5in) ribbon, measuring points B 3cm (1¼in) from point A. Stitch at top of centre front join.

9. Stitch pompon (see Trimmings: page 9) at back, over lower edge of tunic.

10. To make his straw hat, place two strands of raffia together and tie a knot at one end. Holding the cut end underneath, wrap the section of raffia next to the knot smoothly round it, stitching it to the knot with a thin strand of raffia. Continue round and round (see diagram page 41), until you have made a flat circle 6cm (2⅜in) in diameter; then turn at right angles and continue straight down to make the sides of the crown 1.5-2cm (¾in) deep. Turn outwards again for the brim, finishing off when it is about 1.5cm (⅝in) wide, making the diameter of the hat about 9cm (3½in).

11. Knot ends of elastic and stitch at each side, inside crown, so that it fits comfortably under his chin.

12. Glue ribbon round crown, join at back. Fold 7cm (2¾in) ribbon in half and glue at centre back, to hang down over brim. Trim cut ends neatly.

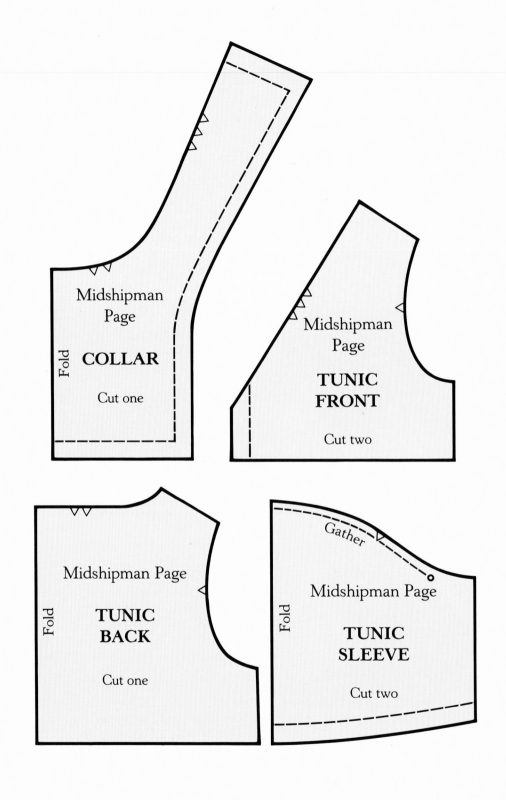

Midshipman
Page

COLLAR

Fold

Cut one

Midshipman
Page

**TUNIC
FRONT**

Cut two

Midshipman Page

**TUNIC
BACK**

Fold

Cut one

Gather

Midshipman Page

**TUNIC
SLEEVE**

Fold

Cut two

BRIDESMAIDS
VIOLET AND PRIMROSE

A quick and simple little dress to make — but very effective. For identical bridesmaids, you could make two dresses from 20cm (8in) fabric. A few tiny flowers between the ears to match the lace-edged posy provide a dainty finishing touch.

MATERIALS

20cm (8in) silver-grey fur fabric, 70cm (27in) wide
5 x 10cm (2 x 4in) grey felt (to tone with fur)
3cm (1¼in) square black felt
Polyester stuffing
Matching threads
Scraps of stiff card or plastic (double cereal carton or cottage cheese tub lid)
Clear adhesive

20cm (8in) pink-and-white or blue-and-white lightweight cotton-type fabric, 45cm (18in) wide, for the dress
1.2m (1⅜yd) pink-and-white or blue-and-white lace, 10mm (⅜in) deep
50cm (½yd) pink or blue satin ribbon, 1.5mm (¹/₁₆in) wide
20cm (¼yd) pink or blue satin ribbon, 3mm (⅛in) wide
20cm (¼yd) pink or blue feather-edge satin ribbon, 9mm (⅜in) wide
Tiny pink or blue artificial flowers
25cm (10in) matching bias binding
20cm (¼yd) narrow round elastic
Matching threads
Florists' stem binding (optional)
Clear adhesive (as above)

1. Use the pattern pieces for the Junior Rabbit (page 104). In grey fur fabric, cut the head gusset once; cut the face, body and leg twice each, and the arm (reverse two) and ear four times. Cut the sole twice in felt; then cut it again slightly smaller, following the broken line, in card or stiff plastic. Mark notches.

2. Turn to page 100 and follow the directions for the 'all-fur' version of the basic Adult Rabbit (omitting the mouth).

3. Cut the dress and collar once each in fabric.

4. Bind the armhole edges, stretching the binding as you do so.

5. Join the centre back seam.

6. Turn under the top edge along the broken line, turn the raw edge narrowly under and stitch.

7. Thread very narrow ribbon through these channels, bringing the ends out at the centre back. Fit dress on rabbit and draw up round neck.

8. Turn up hem to length and herringbone-stitch over the raw edge. Then trim with lace so that it slightly overlaps the lower edge.

9. Join the centre back seam of the collar.

10. Turn under the top edge along the broken line, turn the raw edge narrowly under and stitch.

11. Turn the raw lower edge under and tack. Pin lace so that it slightly overlaps the lower edge, as hem of dress, then stitch into place.

12. Thread elastic through the top channel and draw up to fit around the neck, over the dress.

13. Bunch a few flowerheads together for her head-dress, and bind the stems with thread (or fine wire) and stem binding if available. Knot the centre of the feather-edge ribbon around the stems, then stitch to the head as illustrated, so that the flowers are between her ears and the ribbon hangs down at the back. Trim the cut ends in an inverted V-shape.

14. Bunch more flowerheads together for her posy, and bind the stems securely. Then gather a 25cm (10in) length of lace and draw up to form a frill round the posy, catching it into position behind the flowers. Knot 3mm (⅛in) ribbon around the stems to hang down as illustrated. Stitch to her paw.

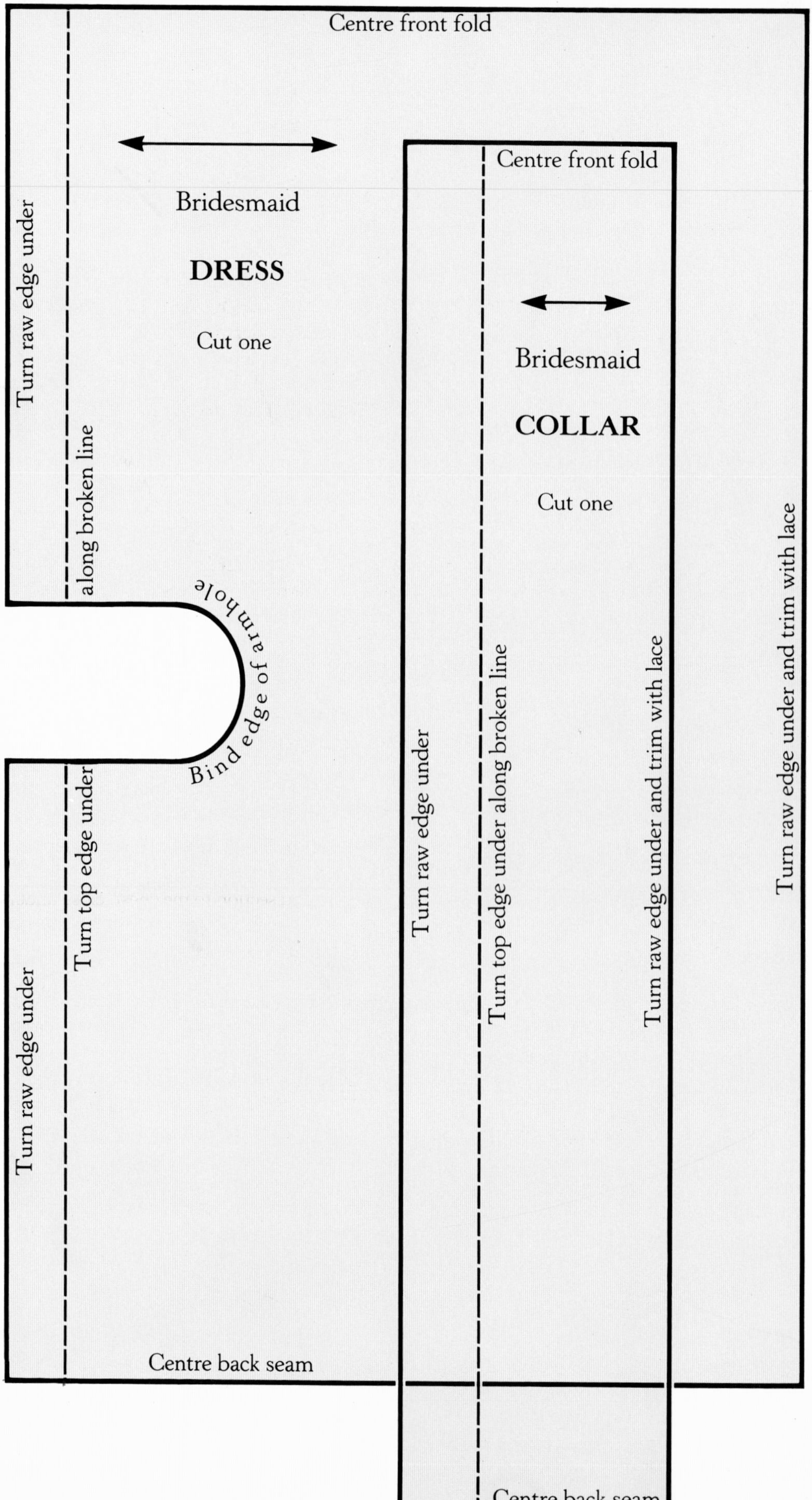

Centre front fold

Turn raw edge under

along broken line

Bridesmaid

DRESS

Cut one

Centre front fold

Bridesmaid

COLLAR

Cut one

Bind edge of armhole

Turn top edge under

Turn raw edge under

Turn raw edge under

Turn top edge under along broken line

Turn raw edge under and trim with lace

Turn raw edge under and trim with lace

Centre back seam

Centre back seam

BARLEYCORN
BROWN

Determined to match the ▨▨▨▨ her attendants on
the Big Day, Barleycorn ▨▨▨▨ ▨ooked so elegant.
His splendid waistcoat a ▨▨▨▨ cravat were carefully chosen to enhanc ▨▨▨▨ rey suit, which is
edged with matching ▨▨▨▨ his is the kind of
narrow dress or lamps ▨▨▨▨ t can be cut down
the centre (see page ▨▨▨▨ ld use plaited ribbon braid instead ▨▨▨▨

His waistcoat is m ▨▨▨▨ a lightweight patterned fabric to felt ▨▨▨▨ almost as good if
you use a medium ▨▨▨▨ nd simply back it
with iron-on non- ▨▨▨▨ (Vilene). And of
course, if you don ▨▨▨▨ onding at all, just
give him a plain ▨ ▨▨▨▨ contrasting felt.

MATERIALS

30cm (12in) cam▨▨▨ ▨▨▨▨in) wide
10cm (4in) crea▨ ▨▨▨▨in) wide
5 x 10cm (2 x 4 ▨▨▨▨ith fur)
3cm (1¼in) sc▨▨▨▨
Polyester stuf▨▨▨▨
Stranded blac▨▨▨▨
Matching th▨▨▨▨
Scraps of st▨▨▨▨ real carton or
  cottage ▨▨▨▨ ▨▨▨
Clear adhe▨▨▨

20cm (¼▨▨▨▨ ▨▨▨▨) wide
14 x 16c▨▨▨ ▨▨▨▨atterned fabric for
  waist▨▨▨
14 x 16 ▨▨▨▨ onding material (Vilene
  Bor▨▨▨▨ ▨▨▨
1.3m ▨▨▨▨ -8mm (¼in) wide, for suit
  (se▨▨▨▨
25cr▨▨▨▨ 7-8mm (¼in) wide, for
  v▨▨▨▨
10▨▨▨▨ ▨ink satin ribbon, 9mm (⅜in)
  ▨▨▨▨
F▨▨▨▨ ▨nhole
V▨▨▨▨ ▨cm (1½in) diameter for tail (if required)
  ▨▨▨▨ e knitting yarn
▨▨▨▨ e (as above)

1 ▨▨ ne pattern pieces for the Adult Rabbit pages
1 ▨▨▨. In camel fur fabric, cut the head gusset and body

onc▨, the face and leg twice each, and the arm (reverse
two) and ear four times. Cut the body once more in
cream fur (for his chest). Cut the sole twice in felt; then
cut it again slightly smaller, following the broken line,
in card or stiff plastic. Mark notches.

2. Turn to page 100 and follow the directions for the
'all-fur' version of the basic Adult Rabbit.

3. Cut the trouser pattern twice in grey felt. Oversew
each piece together between a-b. Then join the two
pieces together between c-a-c, to form the centre front
and back seams. Turn to the right side.

Glue braid along the fold line at the side of each leg,
turning the cut ends neatly inside. Gather round the
top edge, then fit trousers on rabbit and draw up
round the waist, catching to the body to hold in position.

4. Fold the ribbon in half and crease the fold; open out
and gather with tiny stitches along the fold line —
then gather back, close to the first stitches. Draw up
very tightly and secure. Fold in half again and stitch
the gathered section to the chest, close under the chin;
then take the ribbon smoothly down and catch the cut
ends to the chest.

5. Following the instructions, trace the waistcoat onto
Bondaweb then iron onto fabric; cut out and back with
felt.

Glue the full width of the braid down the centre
front, but divide it in half above and below, and glue
each side over the cut edge of the neck and lower
edges. Alternatively, make 50cm (20in) plaited braid
(see Trimmings: page 8); glue round the edge and
side-by-side down the centre.

Place the waistcoat flat on his chest, taking the side
edges (d-d) smoothly round and pinning them over
the side seams of the body. Take the top points (e)
over the shoulders and round the neck, pinning to the
body just behind the head. Make sure the waistcoat fits
very snugly then stitch the sides and top pieces to the
body, removing the pins.

6. Cut the jacket back once, and the front, sleeve and

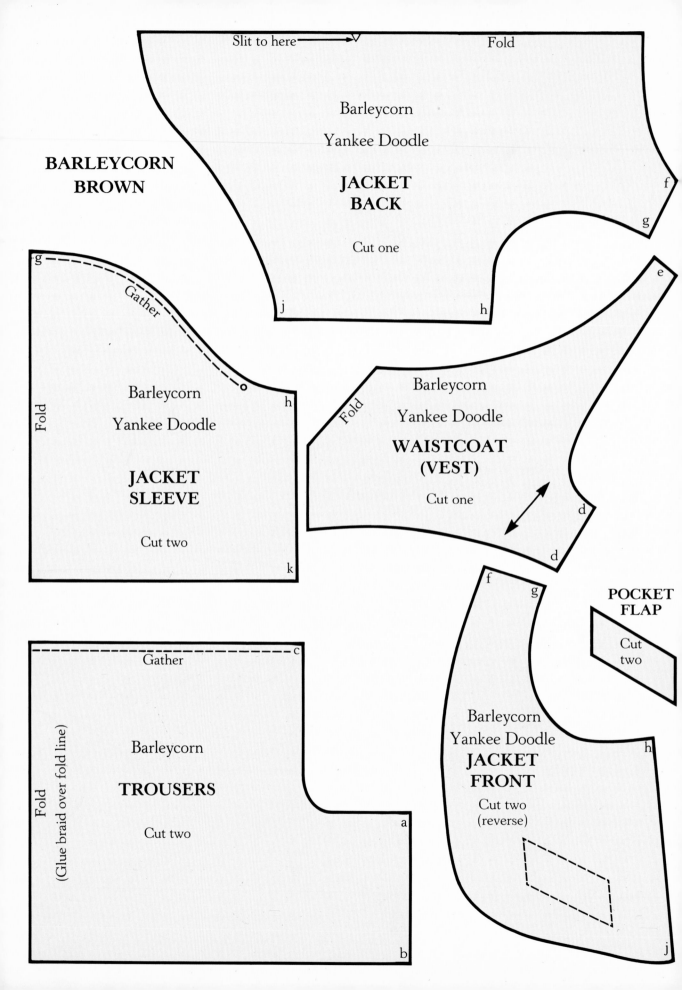

Slit to here →

BARLEYCORN BROWN

Barleycorn

Yankee Doodle

JACKET BACK

Cut one

Fold

f

g

e

g

Gather

Barleycorn

Yankee Doodle

JACKET SLEEVE

Cut two

Fold

h

k

Fold

Barleycorn

Yankee Doodle

WAISTCOAT (VEST)

Cut one

d

d

f

g

POCKET FLAP

Cut two

Barleycorn
Yankee Doodle
JACKET FRONT

Cut two (reverse)

h

j

Gather

c

Fold

(Glue braid over fold line)

Barleycorn

TROUSERS

Cut two

a

b

j

pocket flap twice each, in felt (reverse front). Slit the centre back as indicated.

Oversew the front pieces to the back at each shoulder (f-g).

Gather the top edge of each sleeve between the circles. Fit the sleeves into the armholes, matching the side edges (h) and centre top to the shoulder seam (g). Draw up the gathers to fit, and stitch into place.

Join the side and sleeve seams (j-h-k). Turn to the right side.

Glue braid all round the cut edges, as illustrated, cutting it in half to edge the centre back slit, and also the side and lower edges of the pocket flaps.

Spread a little glue along the top edge of each pocket flap, then stick to the jacket as indicated on the pattern for the front.

7. Stitch the flower (or make a ribbon rose — Trimmings: page 8) into position for his buttonhole.

8. If a tail is required, use either a purchased pompon, or make one as directed on page 9 (Trimmings).

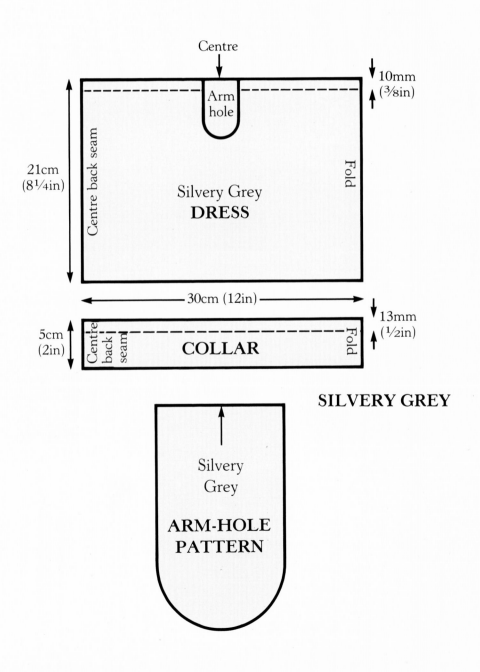

SILVERY

 # GREY

Heart fluttering, and feeling truly romantic in her floating veil and snowy drift of a bridal gown, Silvery Grey is ready to promise her love and devotion to Barleycorn Brown. A lovely present for a little girl — and for a bride, too . . . a special memory of her special day.

The dress is a more sophisticated version of the one the bridesmaids are wearing. As the pattern is too large to fit on the page, there is a diagram from which to draw a larger version of the one on page 50; then use the separate pattern to cut out the armholes. Trim the gown with a heavier, more important lace than the one you use for the bridesmaids — preferably a guipure like the one illustrated.

MATERIALS

30cm (12in) silver-grey fur fabric, 90cm (36in) wide
5 x 10cm (2 x 4in) grey felt (to tone with fur)
3cm (1¼in) square black felt
Polyester stuffing
Matching threads
Scraps of stiff card or plastic (double cereal carton or cottage cheese tub lid)
Clear adhesive
28cm (11in) white spotted voile (dotted Swiss), 60cm (24in) wide
50cm (½yd) fine white net veiling, 65cm (27in) wide
1.8m (2¼yd) guipure lace 10mm (⅜in) deep
70cm (¾yd) white satin ribbon, 1.5mm (1/16in) wide
Bunch of small white artificial flowers for headdress
Small pink rosebuds and white forget-me-nots, etc for her bouquet
35cm (14in) white bias binding
23cm (¼yd) narrow round elastic
Matching threads
Florists' stem binding (optional)
Clear adhesive (as above)

1. Use the pattern pieces for the Adult Rabbit (page 102). In grey fur fabric, cut the head gusset once; cut the face, body and leg twice each, and the arm (reverse two) and ear four times. Cut the sole twice in felt: then cut it again slightly smaller, following the broken line, in card or stiff plastic. Mark notches.

2. Turn to page 100 and follow the directions for the 'all-fur' version of the basic Adult Rabbit (omitting the mouth).

3. The dress pattern is a larger version of the Bridesmaid's Dress (page 50). Prepare your pattern following the measurements shown on the diagram on page 53; mark the centre of the top edge, as indicated. To cut the armhole, trace and cut out the armhole pattern; then place it on the dress pattern as shown on the diagram, top edges level and centres matching — and draw round it. Follow the other diagram to make your collar pattern.

4. Follow the directions for the Bridesmaid's Dress (page 47), steps 3-12 inclusive, but add a second row of lace (step 8) around the hem, just above the first one.

5. Stitch the bunch of white flowers to the top of her head, stems between the ears, bringing a few flower heads forward to form a point over her forehead (see the illustration).

6. Fold the veiling in half so that it measures 50 x 32.5cm (18 x 13½in). Using double thread, gather *along* the fold line; stitch the beginning of the gathers to the back of one ear close to the outer edge at the point where it ceases to be joined to the head. Draw up the gathers to fit across the back of the head, joining the other end to the outer edge of the other ear as before.

7. Bunch the rosebuds and forget-me-nots, etc, together, arranging them to form an attractive bouquet, as illustrated. Bind the stems with thread (or fine wire) and stem binding if available. Stitch to paw.

Baby-Sitting for the Hedgehogs

Mother Hedgehog laid little Hoggy in his cradle. 'He's such a lovely baby!' she smiled to her husband, who gazed into the cradle where his young son lay curled up like a small brush.

Mrs Hedgehog hurried into the kitchen. 'I must get the twins' tea ready,' she said. 'I must collect them from school soon. I wonder how they got on.' It was Holly and Ivy's first day at school, and they had both been looking forward to it.

The door opened and Nanny Prickle came in looking upset. 'My sister has had an accident,' she said tearfully. 'She went for a walk on Blackberry Hill and she was frightened by a sheep. She's very nervous, you know, and when she saw this sheep she curled up into a ball and the next thing she knew she was rolling down the hill, faster and faster. Now she's so dizzy she can only walk in circles.' She turned to Mrs Hedgehog: 'I shall have to go and look after her.'

'I'll come with you', said Mr Hedgehog reassuringly. 'We'll take her to the hospital for an X-ray to make sure she hasn't broken anything.'

'Who will look after little Hoggy while I'm out?' asked Mrs Hedgehog.

'We'll get the pixies to baby-sit,' said Mr Hedgehog.

Flop was delighted. 'What an easy way to earn money,' he laughed.

'As long as the baby behaves itself,' Flip reminded him.

'It's quite a nice little thing,' said Flop thoughtfully, 'for a hedgehog.' Then he sighed. 'I'm bored. I wish they had a television set.'

'Well they haven't,' snapped Flip. 'Why don't you read a book?'

'There's nothing to read,' Flop snapped back.

'Then talk to the baby,' suggested Flip. Flop peered into the cradle: 'Hello!' But Hoggy was asleep.

Mrs Hedgehog had left a big plate of freshly baked buns for the pixies.

'Let's have tea,' said Flop. He picked up two buns and handed one to Flip who looked at it. 'Yours is bigger,' he said.

'No it isn't!' denied Flop. 'And anyway, yours has more currants.'

'It has not!' argued Flip.

'It has!' shouted Flop. 'Look!' And he flung the bun at Flip. Without thinking, Flip threw his bun at Flop, and their bun fight began in earnest. The noise woke little Hoggy, who began to howl.

At that moment Mrs Hedgehog returned with the twins, closely followed by her husband and Nanny Prickle.

Which is why the two pixies spent the rest of the afternoon sweeping up the mess . . . and didn't earn any money for their television set.

MOTHER

HEDGEHOG

Plump and motherly, Mrs Hedgehog has a homely charm that appeals to any age — which means she is likely to become a bestseller if you are marketing the design. And she's an ideal subject to choose if you *are* planning to sell your work, because she is so quick, easy and inexpensive to make.

First turn to page 119 to make the basic Adult Standing Hedgehog: then continue below.

MATERIALS

14 x 60cm (5½ x 24in) striped medium-weight cotton-type fabric for her skirt

White voile or similar lightweight fabric
  35cm (14in) square for the fichu
  22cm (8½in) diameter circle for the mob cap

70cm (⅞yd) lace, 30mm (1¼in) deep

70cm (⅞yd) white bias binding

80cm (1yd) narrow round elastic

Matching threads

1. Join the short edges of the skirt fabric for the centre back seam. Turn under and stitch a 1cm (⅜in) hem around the top edge, turning the raw edge under. Thread elastic through this channel and draw up to fit her waist.

2. Fit the skirt on the animal and turn up the hem to length. Herringbone-stitch over the raw edge.

3. Cut a 35cm (14in) square of voile for the fichu, and a 22cm (8½in) diameter circle for the mob cap.

4. Fold the fichu square diagonally in half; then diagonally in half again, as figure 1. Pin the fabric to hold it exactly together. Points A are the front corners. Measure and mark points B and D following the diagram; then cut away the back corner in a curve as the broken line.

Unpin and open out the second fold only, then re-

pin and join the cut edges, leaving 4cm (1½in) open on the straight edge at one side for turning. Clip the corners and trim the seam closely with pinking shears, then turn to the right side. Close the seam, then top-stitch with tiny stitches very close to the edge.

5. Drape the fichu round her neck, folding and gathering to fit; cross the front corners over as illustrated and bind with thread, then catch to the centre top of her skirt, and then over the top of each paw, to hold in position.

6. Bind the cap, turning the binding over the cut edge. Then, on the right side of the cap, stitch the top edge of the lace over the inner edge of the binding (it won't lie flat — don't worry).

7. Thread elastic through the binding and draw up to fit. Catch the cap lightly to her head to hold it in place.

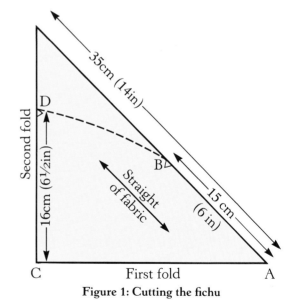

Figure 1: Cutting the fichu

FATHER HEDGEHOG

His smartly braided jacket allows for a generous fit over his comfortable paunch, and he adds a sporty touch with a silk cravat. Dressing Dad is so quick and easy, but the finished result is an amusing toy with considerable personality.

Try to find a silky lampshade or dress braid that you can cut down the centre to make two very narrow strips, to trim the armholes and pockets. If you can't find a suitable braid, use plaited ribbon (Trimmings: page 8) for this purpose.

First turn to page 119 to make the basic Adult Standing Hedgehog: then continue below.

MATERIALS

25cm (10in) square of olive green felt
1.3m (1½yd) matching braid, 6-8mm (¼in) wide (see above)
10cm (4in) square of lightweight silky fabric for his contrasting cravat
3 snap fasteners
Matching threads
Clear adhesive

1. Cut the jacket twice (reverse second piece) in felt; cut out the armholes.

2. Oversew the centre back seam and press open.

3. Stitch snap fasteners inside centre front opening at (o)s.

4. Beginning at the top, and ending at the bottom, of the inside centre front opening, glue braid all round the cut edge of the jacket. Cut the braid in half (or make a very narrow braid as above) and use it to edge the armholes.

5. Cut two pocket flaps and trim the sides and lower edge with very narrow braid. Glue to the jacket front as indicated by the broken lines on the pattern.

6. Fit the jacket on the hedgehog, but pull the fronts back to reveal his chest. Fold the cravat fabric in half diagonally, then drape it *loosely* across his neck, as illustrated; fold the corners under so that the cravat ends

Figure 1: CRAVAT

at each side, level with the edge of the fur where it joins the chest. Catch the folded side edges of the cravat to the animal at this point, between the head and paw.

7. Fasten the front of the jacket, tucking the cravat neatly inside.

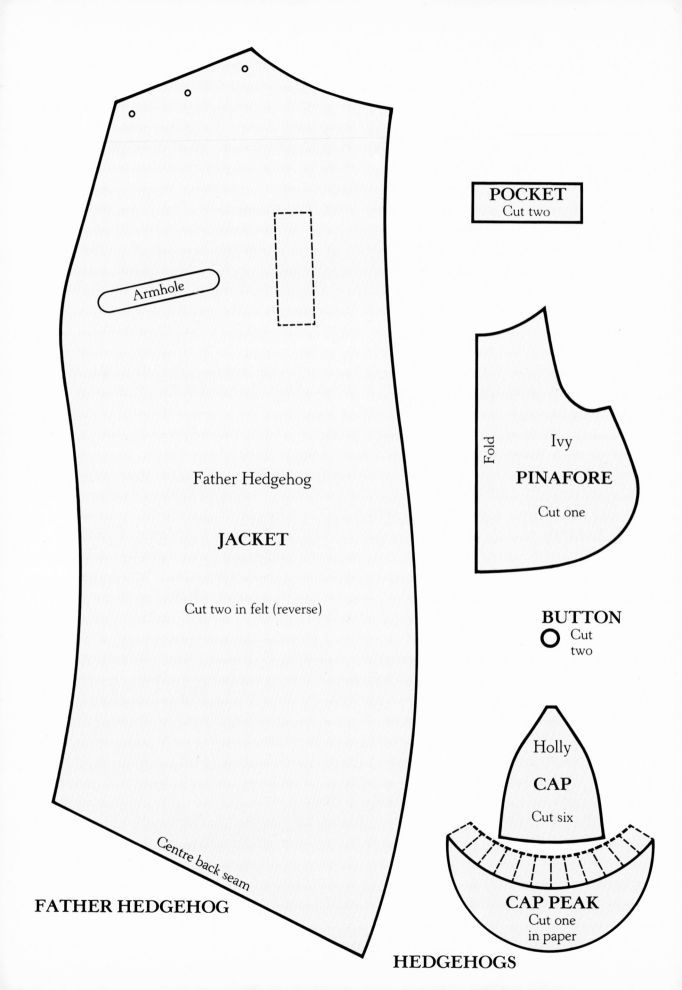

POCKET
Cut two

Armhole

Father Hedgehog

JACKET

Cut two in felt (reverse)

Centre back seam

FATHER HEDGEHOG

Fold

Ivy

PINAFORE

Cut one

BUTTON
Cut two

Holly

CAP

Cut six

CAP PEAK
Cut one
in paper

HEDGEHOGS

HOLLY AND IVY

HEDGEHOG

Two more examples showing how easy it is to create character with very little effort. Mrs Hedgehog shed a tear when she saw her young son looking so grown-up in his new school uniform. But a more cynical eye would judge Hedgehog Junior well able to take care of himself on his first day at school! In contrast, his twin sister wears a demure Victorian pinafore, with a big bow on her head . . . and you wouldn't have thought it possible a hedgehog could have so much feminine charm.

First turn to page 119 to make the basic Junior Standing Hedgehog (A); then continue below.

HOLLY HEDGEHOG

MATERIALS

10cm (4in) square of red felt
5 x 10cm (2 x 4in) green felt
Lightweight woollen fabric for his scarf:
   4.5cm (1¾in) x approximately 40cm (16in)
Scrap of stiff paper (red, if available)
Matching threads
Dry-stick adhesive (optional)
Clear adhesive

1. Cut the cap section three times in each felt. Cut the peak in stiff paper (ignoring the broken lines) and glue it to the red felt (using a glue-stick if you have one). Cut the felt level with the edge of the paper: this will be the top-side of the peak. Turn the peak over and glue the under-side to felt, but this time cut level with the paper along the outer edge of the curve only. Cut the felt 6-8mm (¼-⅜in) away from the inner edge, as the broken line on the pattern, then snip the surplus into tiny tabs, as indicated.

2. Alternating the colours, oversew the six sections of the cap together along the side edges; take care to have them meet neatly at the centre.

3. Fit the inner edge of the peak level with the edge of the cap, centred with a red section, then glue the tabs up inside the cap with clear adhesive.

4. Cut the tiny circle twice in red felt (using a hole punch if you have one). Glue one circle over the joins at the centre of the cap, then glue the other one on top.

5. Following the pattern on your fabric, cut the scarf about 4.5cm (1¾in) wide and the length required (see above).

   Draw threads from each long edge to prevent fraying, and from the short ends to form a fringe about 1cm (⅜in) deep.

6. Knot the scarf round the hedgehog's neck, and fix the cap on his head, as illustrated.

IVY HEDGEHOG

MATERIALS

8 x 10cm (3¼ x 4in) medium-weight printed cotton fabric
8 x 10cm (3¼ x 4in) lightweight iron-on non-woven
   interlining (Vilene)
50cm (½yd) narrow lace — about 10mm (⅜in) deep
20cm (8in) single-face satin ribbon, 15mm (⅝in) wide
Matching threads

1. Iron the interlining onto the back of your fabric, then cut the pinafore.

2. Stitch gathered lace neatly behind the side and lower edges of the pinafore skirt. Stitch a little more gathered lace around the neck edge, on the right side, to form a collar.

3. Catch the four corners of the pinafore securely to the animal, above and below the paws.

4. Make the ribbon into a butterfly bow (Trimmings: page 8), marking points B 6cm (2⅜in) from A. Stitch to the top of her head, as illustrated. Trim the cut ends in an inverted V-shape.

NANNY

PRICKLE

The cap and apron make the Hedgehogs' nursemaid an endearing little creature to give to a friend as a caring mascot. This is an excellent example of how little it takes to give a simple soft toy a personality.

First turn to page 119 to make the basic Adult Standing Hedgehog: then continue below:

MATERIALS

16cm (6¼in) white spotted voile (dotted Swiss), 12.5cm (5in) wide
70cm (¾yd) very narrow white guipure lace
1m (1¼yd) white ribbon, 9mm (⅜in) wide
Matching threads

1. Cut the apron, bib and cap once each in fabric.

2. Turn under and stitch a very narrow hem around the sides and bottom of the apron, and around the sides and top edge of the bib. Then trim with lace, easing it round the corners as necessary so that it lies quite flat.

3. Gather across the top edge of the apron. Pin the top corners directly under each paw, then draw up the gathers across her tummy: remove and secure.

4. Cut a 70cm (30in) length of ribbon and find the centre. Place the apron right side up and pin the ribbon (also right side up) over the gathered top edge, centres matching, and stitch the lower edge of the ribbon over the gathers, distributing them evenly underneath.

5. Place the lower edge of the bib behind the top edge of the ribbon, centres matching, and stitch as before.

6. Tie the apron round her waist, catching the top edge of the bib to her front to hold it in place.

7. Turn under and stitch a narrow hem all round the edge of the cap, then trim with lace as before.

8. Make a butterfly bow (Trimmings: page 8) at the centre of the remainder of the ribbon, measuring points B 3.5cm (1⅜in) from A. Stitch at the centre back of the cap so that the streamers hang down behind. Trim the cut ends in an inverted V-shape. Catch the cap lightly to the top of her head.

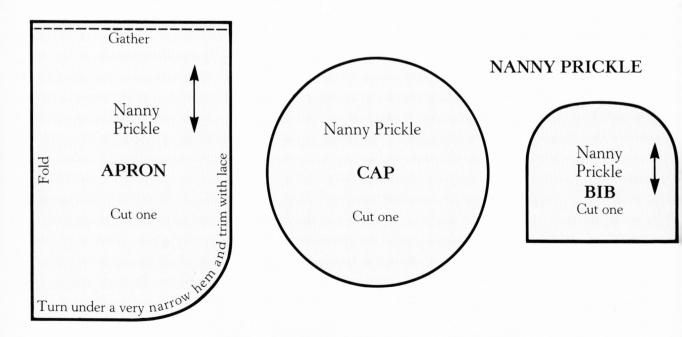

Gather

Nanny Prickle

APRON

Cut one

Fold

Turn under a very narrow hem and trim with lace

Nanny Prickle

CAP

Cut one

NANNY PRICKLE

Nanny Prickle **BIB**
Cut one

BABY HOGGY'S CRADLE

A very special cradle for a very small hedgehog (directions to make the Baby Hedgehog are on page 122). Or a tiny doll, of course. Prettily draped, and romantically trimmed with lace and ribbon and flowers: the part you can't see could be an empty cornflakes carton!

Check that the card is flexible enough to curve round for the sides of the cradle. For stiff card, glue two or three pieces of cereal carton together.

Measure your pieces of card very accurately, and use a sharp craft knife with a metal rule to cut them.

MATERIALS
40cm (½yd) light-to-medium-weight pale lilac dress
   fabric, 90cm (36in) wide

Lightweight wadding: 11 x 14cm (4¼ x 5½in) and 2.5 x
   60cm (1 x 24in)
Stiff card (double- or treble-thickness cereal carton)
Medium-weight card (single-thickness cereal carton)
1.7m (1⅞yd) white lace, 15mm (⅝in) deep
50cm (½yd) white silky braid, 8-10mm (¼-⅜in) wide
30cm (12in) single-face satin ribbon, 15mm (⅝in) wide,
   to tone with fabric
11cm (4¼in) single-face satin ribbon, 9mm (⅜in) wide,
   to tone with fabric
A few toning tiny artificial flowers (forget-me-nots, etc)
Very thin stick, 26cm (10¼in) long
Matching threads
Adhesive tape
Clear adhesive

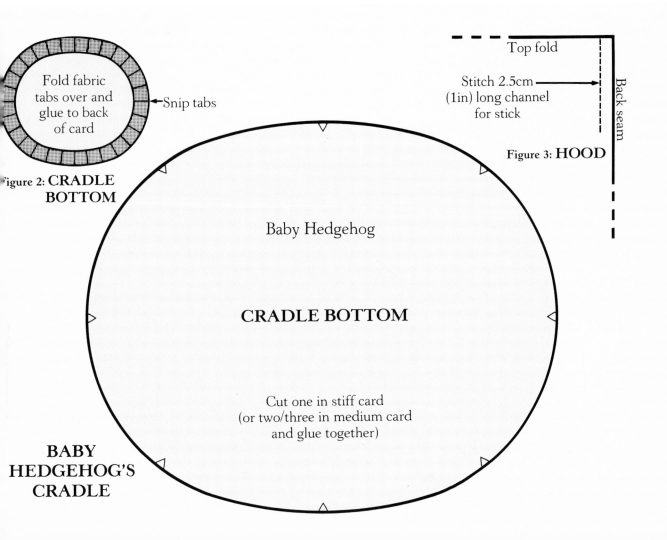

Fold fabric
tabs over and
glue to back
of card

←Snip tabs

Figure 2: **CRADLE
   BOTTOM**

Top fold

Stitch 2.5cm ⟶
(1in) long channel
for stick

Back seam

Figure 3: **HOOD**

Baby Hedgehog

CRADLE BOTTOM

Cut one in stiff card
(or two/three in medium card
and glue together)

**BABY
HEDGEHOG'S
CRADLE**

1. First prepare a really firm base to support your cradle, using very stiff card. Cut two pieces for the sides and two pieces for the ends, as figure 1. Tape firmly together, with the ends *between* the sides. Now cut a piece of card to cover the top; this will be 10cm (4in) x approximately 7cm (2¾in), but measure to be accurate. Tape this securely on top of the sides and ends.

Glue some more pieces of card inside the base to strengthen and add weight.

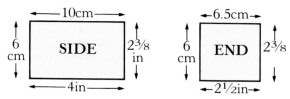

Figure 1: BASE

2. To make the bottom of your cradle, trace the oval pattern onto stiff card and cut it out. Glue wadding on top and trim level with the edge of the card.

Place your fabric absolutely flat, right side down; place the oval on top, wadding side down. Cut the fabric about 15mm (½in) outside the edge of the card, then snip the surplus into tiny tabs (figure 2). Bring the tabs smoothly up, draw them over the edge of the card and glue them to the back.

3. Glue the cradle bottom very firmly to the top of the base.

4. Cut a strip of fabric 7 x 60cm (2¾ x 24in) to line the inside of the cradle. Rule a line on the wrong side 1.5cm (⅝in) from the lower edge, and another 2cm (¾in) from the top edge. Join the short ends of the strip and press the seam open. Gather along the lower line. Mark this edge into eight equal sections; mark the edge of the padded oval into eight also (notches on pattern). Right sides together, pin the gathers round the edge of the oval, matching the marked points; draw up to fit and catch the lining securely to the edge of the oval.

Gather along the upper line, but don't draw up yet.

5. Cut single card 9 x 40cm (3½ x 16in) for the inner sides of the cradle. Fit strip snugly round cradle bottom and mark overlap; remove and glue join.

6. Glue a 2.5 x 40cm (1 x 16in) strip of wadding round the inside of the card, top edges level; trim off the overlap.

Slide the sides down over cradle base.

Pull the lining up over the card, then pull it down over the outside, pinning to hold. Draw up gathers round the outside and oversew lining to top edge of card, distributing the gathers evenly.

7. Cut a piece of fabric 11cm (4¼in) deep x 60cm (24in) for the skirt; to avoid bulk there is no hem allowance, so try to cut along the thread of the fabric — or allow extra if a hem is necessary.

On the wrong side, rule a line 1cm (⅜in) from the top edge. Join the side edges and press the seam open. Gather along the line. Mark this edge into eight, as before. Mark the top edge of the cradle into eight also.

Right side of fabric inside, turn the skirt upside down and slip the gathered edge down over the outside of the cradle until the gathering line is level with the top edge; pin the gathers to the lining, then draw up evenly and catch to hold.

8. Cut another 9 x 40cm (3½ x 16in) piece of card for the outer sides. Fit this tightly round the outside; glue and tape the overlap. Bring the skirt down over the card. Adjust the length, then trim the lower edge with lace.

9. Push the stick down between the two layers of card at the head end of the cradle. Anchor at the bottom with glue, and by stitching the edges of the card together.

10. Glue braid around the top edge of the cradle.

11. Cut a piece of fabric 20 x 60cm (8 x 24in) for the hood. Fold it in half to measure 20 x 30cm (8 x 12in). The fold is the top of the hood, so join the fabric at one side to form the centre back seam (make a flat seam for neatness). Stitch a narrow channel, about 2.5cm (1in) long, alongside the top of the seam, to fit the stick (figure 3).

12. Mark the fold line, then open out and gather along it with large stitches (8-10mm: ⅜in). Draw up temporarily and fit over the top of the stick to determine the length; adjust if necessary. Stitch lace over all the cut edges.

Draw up the top gathers tightly and catch together.

13. Fit hood on top of stick. Make a butterfly bow (Trimmings: page 8) from wider ribbon (mark points B 7cm (2¾in) from A). Catch flowers at centre of bow, then stitch to top of hood.

14. Make narrow ribbon into another butterfly bow, marking points B 3cm (1⅛in) from A. Stitch over braid at foot of cradle.

The Hallowe'en Fancy Dress Ball

Every year a fancy dress ball was held in the village hall to celebrate Hallowe'en. Everyone in Blackberry Hollow tried to dream up the most original costume. All through October they had worked late into the night, secretly cutting and stitching their outfits. Now the 31st had finally arrived, and they were all bubbling with excitement.

Flip and Flop were decorating the village hall for the event. They hung up great armfuls of ivy and hollowed out lots of pumpkins. Then they cut out the eyes and nose and mouth in each pumpkin and stuck a candle inside to make Jack o'Lanterns.

Flip stood back to admire their handiwork. 'It looks good!' he said with satisfaction. 'We won't light the candles until it gets dark.'

Flop agreed. 'It's the best job we've done yet,' he announced.

'Perhaps we'll earn some money this time,' said Flip hopefully. 'We haven't made a penny so far.'

'We'll never get our television set,' Flop moaned.

'Let's hope we make a start tonight,' said Flip encouragingly. Flop nodded, with a heavy sigh.

As it grew dark the guests began to arrive. They all admired the decorations, and the pixies accepted their compliments with broad grins.

'It's a little difficult to see,' murmured Silvery Brown to her husband.

'Could we have some light?' Barleycorn asked.

'This is the big moment!' Flip announced. 'Just wait till you see our Jack o'Lanterns. Give me the matches, Flop.'

'I haven't got them,' said Flop, 'I thought you had them.'

'I distinctly told you to bring the matches,' muttered Flip in exasperation. 'Do I have to remember everything?'

'Don't worry!' called Filbert Speedwell calmly, 'I've plenty of matches in the shop. I'll pop over and get a box.'

The guests whispered and giggled in the dark until Filbert returned. He handed the box to the shamefaced pixies, who quickly lit the candles.

The Jack o'Lanterns filled the hall with a warm orange glow, and soon the Hallowe'en ball was in full swing. Everyone had a wonderful time, bobbing for apples, dancing until their feet ached, eating lots of food and drinking too much elderberry wine.

By the end of the evening they had forgotten about the missing matches. So Flip and Flop decided not to remind them.

'We've had a lovely time,' said Flip, 'even if our money-box is still empty.'

YANKEE DOODLE DANDY

Mr Brown

Many years ago, Mr Brown's uncle, Samuel Sweetcorn Brown, settled in America, where he raised a large family. Mr Brown never tires of boasting about his American cousins, so his stars-and-stripes outfit was a natural choice for the ball.

The narrow braid trimming around his jacket is not essential, although it looks smart and helps to hold the shape of the felt. If you cut a wider braid in half (as illustrated) you will need only half the quantity given below. Alternatively you could make plaited braid (Trimmings: page 8).

Turn to pages 100 and 14 for the directions to make Mr Brown (sleeve-and-paw version with shirt as described, but without additional clothes). Then dress him as described below.

MATERIALS

13cm (5in) red/white striped medium-weight cotton-type fabric, 90cm (36in) wide, for his hat and trousers
30cm (12in) square red felt
30cm (12in) square blue felt
50cm (½yd) matching red braid
1.2m (1¼yd) very narrow matching blue braid (optional)
18cm (7in) matching blue single-face satin ribbon, 10mm (⅜in) wide, for bow-tie
30cm (12in) matching blue ribbon, 23mm (1in) wide, for hat-band
4 small silver beads
Self-adhesive silver stars
20cm (¼yd) narrow round black elastic
Large white pompon (optional) (see page 9) *or* fluffy white knitting yarn
Matching threads
20 x 30cm (8 x 12in) thin white card
14 x 23cm (5½ x 9in) medium-weight card (cereal carton, etc)
Dry-stick adhesive
Clear adhesive

1. Use the pattern for Grandpa and Filbert Speedwell's trousers page 89; cut the piece twice in striped fabric, but *don't* cut away the tail section.

2. Join each piece between a-b. Then join the two pieces together between c-a-c, to form the centre front and back seams. Clip the curves.

3. Make a 1cm (⅜in) hem around the waist (herringbone-stitch over the raw edge). Make similar hems around the lower edge of each leg. Turn to the right side.

4. Gather close to the top edge, then fit trousers on the rabbit and draw up round the waist, catching to the body to hold in position. (Alternatively thread elastic through the top hem and draw up to fit.)

5. Make the narrower blue ribbon into a butterfly bow (Trimmings: page 8), measuring points B 5cm (2in) from A. Stitch to the centre of the elastic, then tie around his neck, knot at the back. Trim ends of ribbon and elastic to length.

6. Use the pattern for Barleycorn Brown's wedding waistcoat (vest), cutting it once in red felt. Stitch silver bead 'buttons' equally down the centre front.

7. Fit and stitch into position as for Barleycorn (page 51: step 5 — final paragraph).

8. Use the patterns for Barleycorn's jacket, and follow the directions (page 51: step 6), to make it in blue felt. Trim with narrow braid as described above.

9. Stitch the pompon to back of the jacket, at the top of the slit. (See Trimmings: page 9).

10. Use the pattern pieces for Mrs Mole's hat to make his top-hat *but increase height of side strip to 8cm (3in)*.
Follow Mrs Mole's directions (page 78: step 5). Cover the brim and crown with red felt, but use the striped fabric to cover the side strip; when doing this allow an extra 1.5cm (½in) of fabric along the two long edges, then fold this surplus neatly over the edge of the card and glue to the back.

11. Glue red braid around the outer edge of the brim, to neaten.
Glue the wider blue ribbon round for his hat-band, then decorate it with silver stars.

68

FILBERT THE PIRATE

When serving in the village shop becomes tedious, Filbert occupies himself with secret dreams of sailing the Seven Seas as a swashbuckling pirate captain. So tonight is his big moment.

Make the basic Adult Squirrel as directed on page 105, then dress him as described below.

MATERIALS
20 x 50cm (8 x 20in) purple felt for coat
25cm (10in) square blue felt for breeches and coat
17 x 20cm (6½ x 8in) black felt for boots
25cm (10in) square black felt for hat and patch
8cm (3in) square white felt for hat
3 x 24cm (1¼ x 9½in) bright pink felt for cummerbund
25cm (10in) square lightweight fabric for neckerchief
80cm (⅞yd) black braid, 10mm (⅜in) wide, for coat and hat
50cm (½yd) olive green braid, 6-8mm (¼in) wide, for cummerbund
80cm (⅞yd) very narrow gold braid for coat
30cm (12in) black narrow round elastic
25cm (10in) square thin card or very stiff paper
10cm (4in) square iron-on bonding material (Vilene Bondaweb or iron-on Vilene) (optional)
Matching threads
Dry-stick adhesive
Clear adhesive

1. Cut the coat back once and the front and sleeve twice each, in purple felt. Cut the breeches, the pocket and the cuff, twice each in blue felt. Cut the boot and sole twice each in black felt. Cut the cummerbund once in pink felt.

2. Open out both breeches pieces and cut away the tail section at one corner only (reverse the second piece).
Gather the lower edge of each piece; then pin to the top edge of a boot, matching the side edges (b) and notches. Draw up the gathers to fit and oversew together.
Join the side edges between a-n.
Stitch a sole to the bottom of each boot, matching the notches and seam.
Join the two pieces between c-a-d to form the centre

front and back seams (c-a-c for the rabbit). Turn to the right side.

3. For the squirrel, gather the top edge between e-e, then fit boots and breeches on squirrel and draw up round the waist, catching the back corners (e-e) securely together with a thread taken from side to side through the tail several times (use a darning needle).
For the rabbit, gather round the top edge, then fit breeches on rabbit and draw up round the waist, catching to the body to hold in position.

4. Glue olive braid along both long edges of the cummerbund. Then fit round his waist, over the top edge of his breeches, and catch the ends securely at each side of the tail.

5. Cut the edges of the neckerchief along the straight of the fabric, then draw a few threads along each edge to prevent fraying. Fold in half diagonally and knot tightly round his neck as illustrated.

6. Oversew the front pieces of his coat to the back at each shoulder (h-j). Gather the top edge of each sleeve between the circles. Fit the sleeves into the armholes, matching the side edges (k) and centre top to the shoulder seam (j). Draw up the gathers to fit and stitch into place.
Join the sleeve and side seams (l-k-m). Before turning to the right side, pin a cuff over the bottom of each sleeve, lower edges level (right side of cuff to wrong side of sleeve); match the centre of the cuff to the seam, with the lower corners meeting together at the centre fold of the sleeve (as broken line). Oversew together all round the lower edge.
Turn to the right side and fold the cuff up over the sleeve, then catch the side edges of the cuff together between the lower edge and the notch.
Glue gold braid along the top and side edges of the cuff, as the wavy line (finish the cut ends neatly up inside the sleeve).

7. Glue a length of black braid along the centre front edges and round the neck of the coat.

69

8. Trim each pocket with gold braid as indicated by the wavy line, then glue the top edge to the coat, positioning as the broken line on the pattern.

9. Cut the eye patch in thin card (or stiff paper), then glue it to black felt. Cut the felt level with the card. Make a knot at one end of the elastic and stitch behind one top corner of the patch. Measure elastic round the head and cut to length, then fix the other end behind the other top corner in the same way.

10. Following the solid lines, cut the hat twice in thin card (or stiff paper). Glue to black felt, then cut the felt as the broken lines.

Turn the surplus up over the lower edge on each piece, and glue to the back of the card.

Place the two pieces exactly together and oversew all round the curved edge. Glue black braid over this edge, turning cut ends up inside the hat.

Cut the skull and crossbones in white felt (use Bondaweb, or iron-on Vilene, if you have some) and glue (or bond) to the front as illustrated.

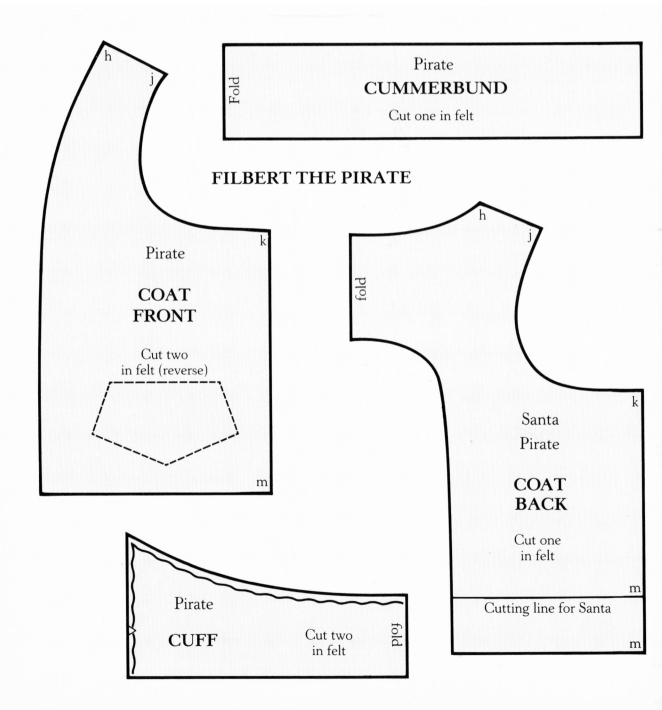

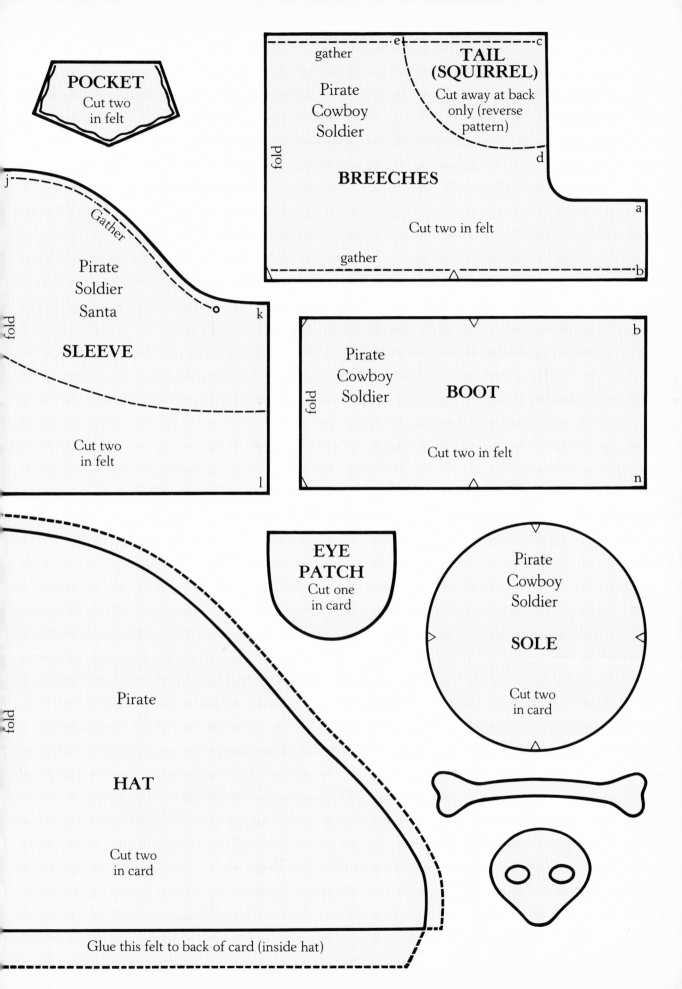

POCKET
Cut two
in felt

TAIL (SQUIRREL)
Cut away at back
only (reverse
pattern)

gather

Pirate
Cowboy
Soldier

BREECHES

Cut two in felt

gather

e

c

d

a

b

Gather

Pirate
Soldier
Santa

SLEEVE

Cut two
in felt

fold

j

k

l

Pirate
Cowboy
Soldier

BOOT

Cut two in felt

fold

b

n

EYE PATCH
Cut one
in card

Pirate
Cowboy
Soldier

SOLE

Cut two
in card

Pirate

HAT

Cut two
in card

fold

Glue this felt to back of card (inside hat)

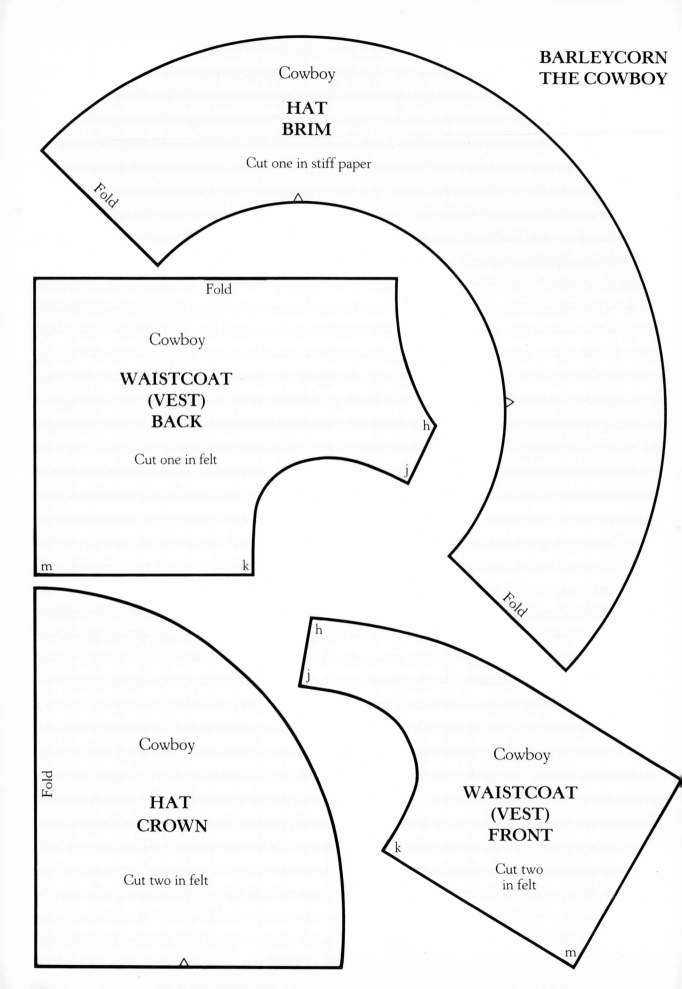

**BARLEYCORN
THE COWBOY**

Cowboy

**HAT
BRIM**

Cut one in stiff paper

Fold

Fold

Cowboy

**WAISTCOAT
(VEST)
BACK**

Cut one in felt

h

j

m   k

h

j

Cowboy

**HAT
CROWN**

Cut two in felt

Fold

Cowboy

**WAISTCOAT
(VEST)
FRONT**

k

Cut two
in felt

m

BARLEYCORN THE COWBOY

Barleycorn's favourite stories are all about the Wild West, so this is his chance to be a cowboy. Silvery lent him her washing line to use as a lassoo; all he needs now is a horse!

Make Barleycorn as directed on page 51, then dress him as below.

MATERIALS

15 x 24cm (6 x 9½in) camel felt for breeches
17 x 20cm (6½ x 8in) mid-brown felt for boots
12 x 30cm (5 x 12in) orange felt for waistcoat (vest)
25 x 60cm (10 x 24in) cream felt for hat
20cm (8in) lightweight check fabric for neckerchief
30cm (12in) dark brown grosgrain ribbon, 15mm (⅝in) wide, for his belt
40cm (15in) striped grosgrain ribbon, 20-25mm (¾-1in) wide, for his hat band
70cm (¾yd) narrow black ric-rac braid
70cm (¾yd) narrow green fancy braid
50cm (½yd) medium-weight piping cord for lassoo
Small (20mm/¾in) gilt buckle for his belt
6 gilt studs, about 9mm (⅜in) diameter, for belt
22cm (8½in) circle of stiff paper
Matching threads
Dry-stick adhesive (or clear adhesive)
Clear adhesive (optional)

1. Using the patterns for Filbert the Pirate's breeches and boots (page 71), cut the breeches twice in camel felt, and the boot and sole twice each in mid-brown. Cut the waistcoat (vest) back once and the front twice, in orange felt.

2. Follow the directions for Filbert's breeches and boots (page 69: steps 2 and 3), ignoring the instruction to cut away the tail section.

3. Fix the buckle at the centre of the brown grosgrain ribbon, then fix three studs at each side, about 1cm (⅜in) apart. Fit round his waist, over the top of his breeches, joining at the back.

4. Cut the edges of the neckerchief along the straight of the fabric, then draw a few threads along each edge to prevent fraying. Fold in half diagonally and knot at back of neck, as illustrated.

5. Oversew the waistcoat (vest) fronts to the back along the shoulder (h-j) and side (k-m) edges. Turn to the right side.

Stitch ric-rac braid all round the front and lower edges, beginning at the back of the neck. Stitch or glue green braid so that it just overlaps the inner edge of the ric-rac.

6. Cut the hat brim in paper and glue it to the cream felt. Cut the felt about 3mm (⅛in) away from the inner and outer edges of the paper. Glue the other side of the paper to the felt and repeat.

Cut the crown twice in felt and join round the curved edge. Matching the notches, oversew to the inner edge of the brim. Turn to the right side.

Top-stitch neatly all round the outer edge of the brim.

Stitch or glue striped ribbon around crown.

7. Wind the piping cord into a circle, as illustrated, and stitch to his paw.

CAPTAIN ACORN
OF THE REGIMENT

If he hadn't been so keen on trains, Acorn Speedwell would have joined the Army. So the Hallowe'en Ball is a splendid opportunity to change his stationmaster's uniform for a military one.

Turn to page 105 to make the basic Adult Squirrel. Then dress him as directed below. If you don't want to plait your own black braid, you could substitute black ric-rac.

MATERIALS

10 x 90cm (4 x 36in) scarlet felt for tunic and helmet
15 x 24cm (6 x 9½in) white felt for breeches
10 x 50cm (4 x 20in) black felt for boots and helmet
18cm (7in) square gold felt for trimmings
6.2m (7yd) black satin ribbon, 1.5mm (¹/₁₆in) wide
1.3m (1½yd) white satin ribbon, 1.5mm (¹/₁₆in) wide
2.25m (2½yd) gold metallic grosgrain ribbon, 1.5mm (¹/₁₆in) wide
50cm (½yd) black braid, about 10mm (³/₈in) wide, to fold round edge of peak, etc
Lace daisy or similar motif, about 2.5cm (1in) diameter, for helmet
25 x 30cm (10 x 12in) thin card
9 x 7cm (3½ x 2¾in) medium card
Scrap of waste stiff card 8cm (3in) deep x about 3cm (1¼in) wide
Matching threads
Dry-stick adhesive (optional)
Clear adhesive

(*Note:* Before cutting out the pieces for the tunic as directed in step 1, check to ensure that you will have a suitable area of red felt left to cut the top and side of the cap: see step 8.)

1. Using the patterns for Filbert the Pirate's breeches and boots (page 71) cut the breeches twice in white felt, and the boot and sole twice each in black. In red felt, cut the tunic front once and the back twice; cut Filbert the Pirate's sleeve twice. Cut the front panel of the tunic, and the helmet trim once each in gold felt, and the cuff and epaulette twice each.

2. Follow the directions for Filbert's breeches and boots (page 69; steps 2 and 3).

3. Oversew the back pieces of his tunic to the front at each shoulder (h-j). Gather the top edge of each sleeve between the circles. Fit the sleeves into the armholes, matching the side edges (k) and centre top to the shoulder seam (j). Draw up the gathers to fit and stitch into place.

Join the sleeve and side seams (l-k-m). Turn to the right side.

4. Mark the horizontal lines in pencil on the front panel. Plait three 40cm (16in) lengths of black ribbon to make braid (see Trimmings: page 8); stitch or glue along each marked line, and along the lower edge, trimming level at each side.

Glue the middle of the panel lightly to the tunic, centres matching, and neck and waist edges level; then appliqué the side edges. Make another length of braid, from three 30cm (12in) lengths of ribbon, and glue over the side edges; turn the cut ends over the waist edge to the wrong side and glue inside tunic.

5. Glue a cuff round the bottom of each sleeve. Make two lengths of plaited braid, each from three 25cm (10in) lengths of black ribbon, and glue over the top edge of each cuff, as illustrated.

6. Make two lengths of plaited braid, each from three 15cm (6in) lengths of black ribbon, and glue them around the curved edge of the epaulettes (as wavy line on pattern). Then glue epaulettes over shoulder seams, straight edge level with neckline.

7. Fit the tunic on the squirrel: overlap and join the centre back edges above the tail, then catch each side securely alongside the tail.

8. Using red felt for the top and side, and black for the peak, make his helmet as directed for Stationmaster Speedwell's cap (page 34; steps 11-15 inclusive) BUT *add 3cm (1¼in) to the depth of the pattern for the side, so that you cut the card 7cm (2¾in) deep instead of 4cm (1½in approx).*

9. Glue black braid round the outer edge of the peak, folding it over the edge. Glue a band of black braid

around the top edge of the helmet.

Make a length of plaited gold braid from three 35cm (14in) lengths of metallic ribbon. Stitch each end inside the lower edge of the helmet, just behind the back corner of the peak, to form the chinstrap. Then make another length of gold braid, from three 40cm (16in) lengths of ribbon, and glue around the lower edge.

Glue the gold felt circle at the centre front of the helmet, 2cm (¾in) below the top edge. Glue the lace motif on top. Plait three 20cm (8in) lengths of black ribbon and trim to measure 10cm (4in). Mark the hel-

met 2.5cm (1in) below the top edge and 2cm (¾in) each side of the gold felt circle: glue the ends of the plait at the marked points, to hang between as illustrated. Make two tassels (see Trimmings: page 9), each from five 10cm (4in) lengths of black ribbon, and glue over the ends of the plait, as illustrated.

Finally, wind the white ribbon evenly around an 8cm (3in) deep piece of stiff card: slide off carefully and bind the centre tightly with matching thread. Then fold in half and bind again, just below fold (as for a tassel, but without knot). Glue to centre front of helmet to protrude over top edge, as illustrated.

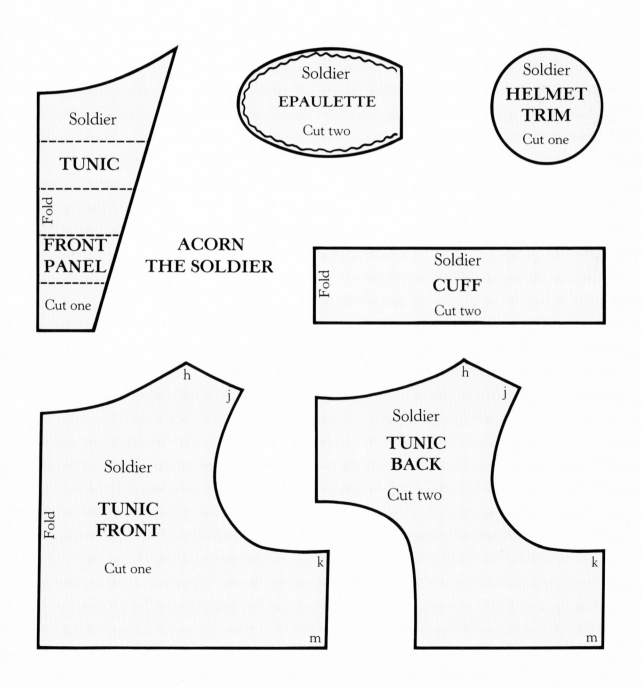

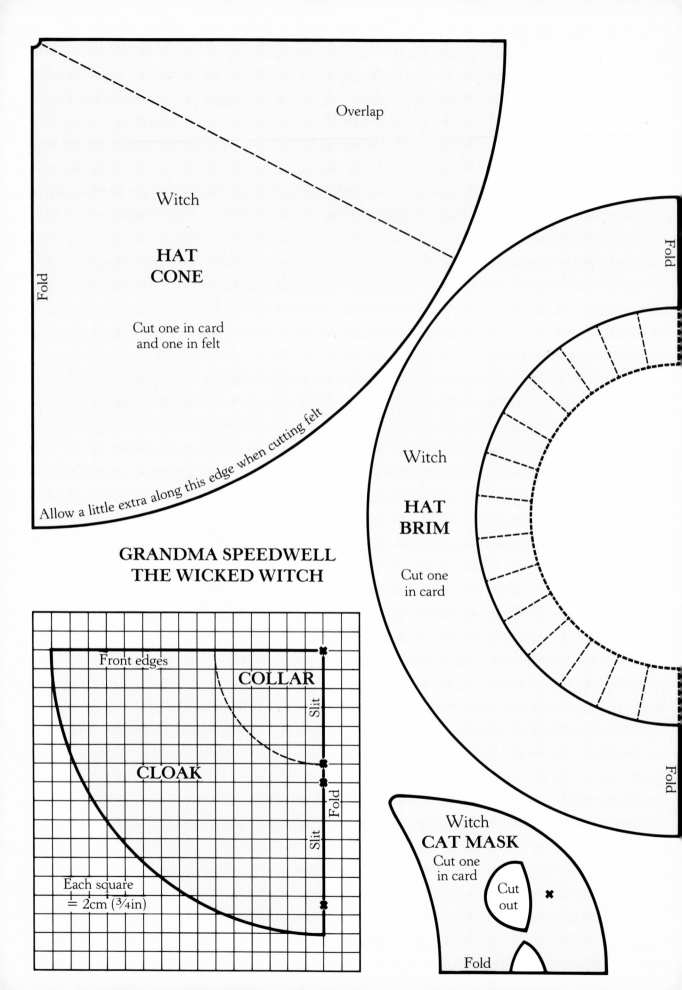

Overlap

Witch

HAT CONE

Cut one in card
and one in felt

Fold

Allow a little extra along this edge when cutting felt

Fold

Witch

HAT BRIM

Cut one
in card

Fold

**GRANDMA SPEEDWELL
THE WICKED WITCH**

Front edges

COLLAR

Slit

CLOAK

Slit

Fold

Each square
= 2cm (¾in)

Witch
CAT MASK

Cut one
in card

Cut
out

Fold

STAR-CROSSED WITCH

Grandma Speedwell

Flip and Flop had a shock when they saw Grandma Speedwell in her witch's outfit; she was so convincing that for a nasty moment they thought Harriet Hemlock had returned. Then they noticed that the witch's faithful black cat was really a baby owl in disguise.

Make and dress Grandma Speedwell as directed on page 91. Then make her cloak and pointed hat as described below.

MATERIALS
40cm (15in) black felt, 90cm (36in) wide
Scrap of pink felt (for cat mask)
30 x 40cm (12 x 16in) thin card (black if possible)
Self-adhesive silver stars
Matching black thread
Elastic band (for cat mask)
Dry-stick adhesive
Clear adhesive

1. Make a pattern for the cloak following the diagram. Cut the side of the hat and the brim (ignoring the broken lines) once each in card. Cut the cloak in felt: but before doing so, make sure you leave a large enough area of felt to cut the hat cone once and the brim twice.

2. Cut two slits between the (x)s, as indicated, in the centre back fold of the cloak, and carefully mark the semi-circular broken line; to do this, cut your pattern along the broken line, then place the collar section on the felt and draw round the curved edge. Gather along the marked line, then fit the cloak on the squirrel and draw up tightly around the neck, securing under her chin. Arrange the points of the collar as illustrated, and fit her tail neatly through the lower slit.

3. Cut the hat cone in felt, leaving a little extra around the lower edge. Curve the card cone round and glue the overlap. Glue the felt smoothly on top and trim off excess around the lower edge.

4. Glue the card brim to felt and cut it level with both edges of the card. Then glue the under-side of the brim to the felt, but this time cut only the outer edge level; leave a surplus overlapping the inner edge as the

broken line on the pattern. Snip this surplus into small tabs, as indicated.

5. Place the cone on the top of the brim and bring the tabs up inside, gluing them firmly all round.

6. Decorate both the cloak and hat with silver stars, as illustrated.

7. To make the cat mask, trace the pattern onto thin card and cut it out, cutting out the eyes very carefully.

8. Glue to black felt, then cut the felt level with the card all round, and cut out the eyes. Cut the nose in pink felt and glue into position.

9. Stitch the elastic band to the back of the mask — at the points marked (x).

OLD MOTHER HUBBARD

Mrs Mole

The Reverend Mole felt it inappropriate for the vicar to attend the Hallowe'en Ball. But nothing could prevent his wife joining the festivities — as Old Mother Hubbard. And she persuaded a young hedgehog to play her hungry dog (Junior Sitting Hedgehog (B): page 122). Turn to page 109 to make the basic Mole, adding spectacles as directed for the Reverend Mole (page 21). Then dress her as described below.

MATERIALS

14 x 60cm (5½ x 24in) blue/white striped fabric for skirt
12 x 15cm (4¾ x 6in) navy blue flowered fabric for apron
20cm (¼yd) mid-blue felt, 90cm (36in) wide, for her cape and hat
60cm (¾yd) blue/white lace, 10mm (⅜in) deep, to trim her skirt
1.5m (1¾yd) heavy navy blue lace, 10mm (⅜in) deep, to trim her cape and hat
1.2m (1⅜yd) white lace, 15mm (½in) deep, to trim her cape and hat
1m (1yd) satin ribbon, 12mm (½in) wide, in *each of three toning colours*, for roses to trim her hat
40cm (½yd) blue sheer-stripe ⎞ or use
  ribbon for hat   ⎟ the
80cm (1yd) green sheer-stripe ⎟ same
  ribbon for hat   ⎠ colour
Snap fastener
Matching threads
6 x 30cm (2¼ x 12in) thin card
14 x 23cm (5½ x 9in) medium-weight card (cereal carton, etc)
Dry stick adhesive
Clear adhesive

1. Follow the directions for Mrs Brown's skirt (page 16: steps 3-5 inclusive).

2. Narrowly hem sides and lower edge of apron fabric. Turn top edge under and gather close to fold; draw up to measure 8cm (3in). Pin, then stitch, over centre front of skirt, top edges level.

3. Pin cape pattern to felt, making sure there is enough left to cut the hat.

4. Stitch navy blue lace, slightly overlapping, around outer edge of the cape (gather to ease around curve).

Tack white lace around the neck edge, straight edges level. Gather lace and felt together, close to the edge; fit on mole and draw up gathers around neck. Sew snap fastener at centre front.

5. Cut the hat brim and crown once each in medium-weight card (ignore broken lines). Cut the side twice in thin card. Cut felt for crown, following outer broken line. Glue card crown in centre of felt circle: then snip out V-shapes to form tiny tabs.

Roll up one side strip of card, fit it inside the brim and allow it to open out to fit snugly; mark the overlap, then remove and glue the join. Place the crown, felt side down, on a flat surface; place side cylinder over it, then bring tabs up and glue round edge of card.

Glue the brim to the felt and cut it level with both edges of the card. Then glue the under-side of the brim to the felt, but this time cut only the outer edge level; leave a surplus overlapping the inner edge as broken line. Snip into tabs, as indicated. Place the crown on top of the brim and glue tabs up inside.

Wrap second card strip round crown and trim off excess. Glue to felt, then trim felt level with one short and both long edges: leave 1cm (⅜in) overlapping remaining edge. Glue neatly round over first strip.

6. Glue navy blue lace around side of the crown, straight edge of lace level with top edge. Glue more lace to outer edge of brim, to hang straight down.

Gather remaining white lace. Draw up and distribute the gathers evenly, stitch (or glue) to under-side of brim, as illustrated.

Fold 25cm (10in) blue ribbon in half and stitch fold to crown, so that the ends hang down at the back. Make a formal bow (Trimmings: page 7) from the remaining ribbon, but don't bind the centre. Stitch or glue over fold.

Make four roses in each shade (Trimmings: page 8), from 30cm (12in) lengths of ribbon. Glue evenly round the hat, as illustrated.

Take the green ribbon over the top of the hat and tie under the chin. Trim cut ends of the streamers and ties in an inverted V-shape.

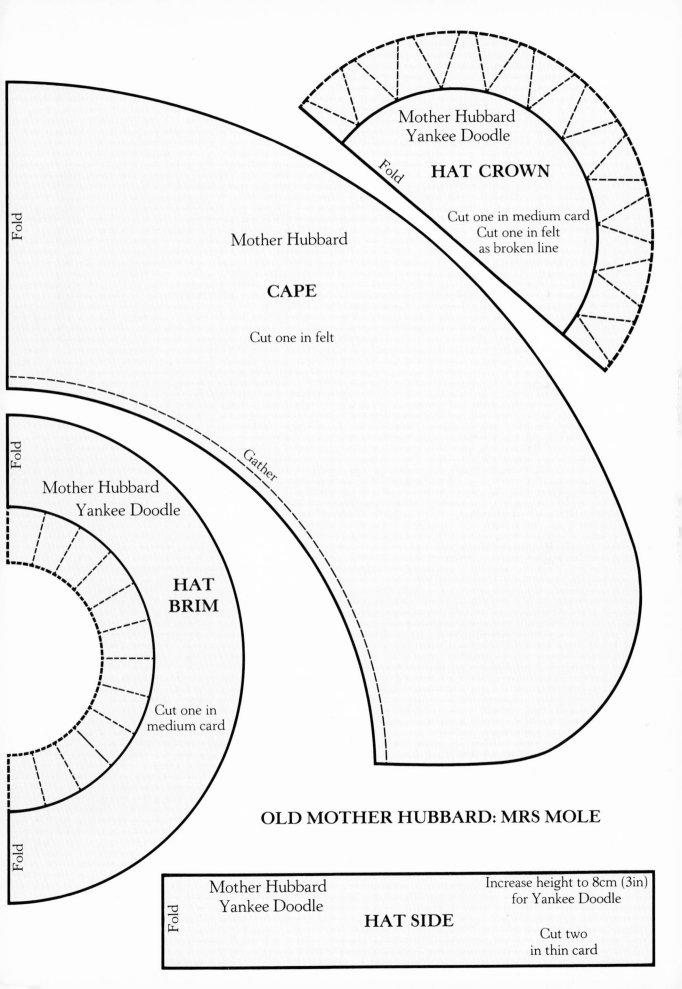

HAT CROWN

Mother Hubbard
Yankee Doodle

Fold

Cut one in medium card
Cut one in felt
as broken line

Mother Hubbard

CAPE

Cut one in felt

Fold

Gather

HAT BRIM

Mother Hubbard
Yankee Doodle

Fold

Cut one in
medium card

Fold

OLD MOTHER HUBBARD: MRS MOLE

Mother Hubbard
Yankee Doodle

Fold

Increase height to 8cm (3in)
for Yankee Doodle

HAT SIDE

Cut two
in thin card

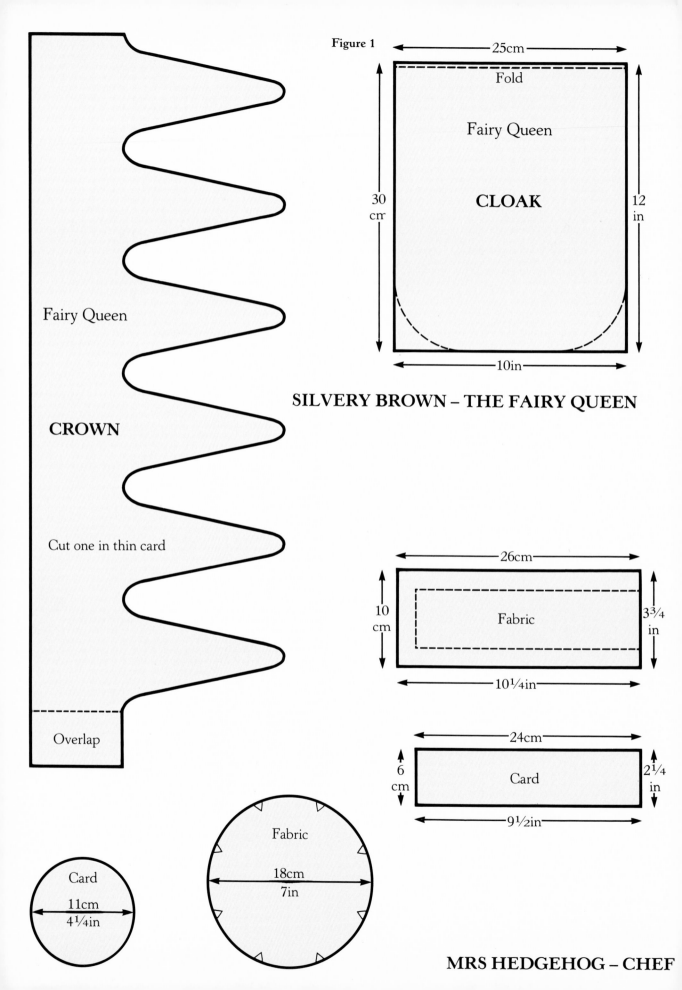

Figure 1

Fairy Queen

CROWN

Cut one in thin card

Overlap

25cm

Fold

Fairy Queen

CLOAK

30 cm

12 in

10in

SILVERY BROWN – THE FAIRY QUEEN

26cm

Fabric

10 cm

3¾ in

10¼in

24cm

Card

6 cm

2¼ in

9½in

Card

11cm

4¼in

Fabric

18cm

7in

MRS HEDGEHOG – CHEF

THE FAIRY QUEEN

Silvery Brown

Barleycorn Brown's young bride isn't just pretty; she's practical too! Her new husband was most impressed when, instead of asking him for a new dress to wear to the ball, she used Christmas tree decorations to transform her wedding gown into the glittering royal robes of the Fairy Queen.

Turn to page 54 to make Silvery and her wedding dress. Then complete the outfit as directed below.

MATERIALS

25 x 60cm (10 x 24in) fine white net veiling
10 x 45cm (4 x 17in) or 15 x 22cm (6 x 8½in) white
    spotted voile (dotted Swiss) (as dress fabric)
90cm (1yd) length of silver tinsel
1.7m (2yd) length of silver ball Christmas tree decoration
    (balls about 7mm (¼in) diameter)
80cm (1yd) white taffeta or satin ribbon, 35-40mm
    (1½in) wide
3.6m (4yd) white satin ribbon, 1.5mm (¹⁄₁₆in) wide
Matching white thread
8 x 20cm (3 x 8in) thin white card
Dry-stick adhesive
Clear adhesive

1. Stitch two rows of silver balls around the hem of her dress, one immediately above each row of lace.

2. Fold the net in half to measure 25 x 30cm (10 x 12in), then pin the cut edges together, keeping the two layers of net absolutely flat, and round off the lower corners as figure 1.

Tack net, then stitch tinsel all round the cut edges, beginning and ending at each end of the fold.

Gather across the top edge of the cloak, close to the fold; draw up to measure about 13cm (5in)

Cut the ribbon in half, gather one end of each piece and stitch behind the tinsel at the top corners of the cloak to form ties. Trim the cut ends in an inverted V-shape.

3. Trace the crown pattern onto thin card and cut out.

Glue the dress fabric to the front of the card and trim level all round. Cover the back of the card with fabric in the same way.

Make a length of plaited braid (Trimmings: page 8) from three 90cm (1yd) lengths of narrow white ribbon. Glue braid all round the top edge of the crown, taking it very neatly round the curves and points, overlapping just enough to hide the cut edge of the fabric.

Curve round into a circle and glue the overlap at the centre back.

Make another length of plaited braid, from three 30cm (12in) lengths of ribbon, and glue around the lower edge of the crown.

Stitch two rows of silver balls around the crown, immediately above the braid.

Cut six balls off the string and glue one to each top point, as illustrated.

THE MASTER CHEF

Mrs Hedgehog

Famous throughout Blackberry Hollow for her hedgehog pudding, Mrs Hedgehog has long nursed a secret ambition to open her own high-class teashop. There the customers would feast on feather-light scones with whipped cream and bramble jelly, honey-topped blackberry buns, wild strawberry gateau, and hedgerow fruit salad with blackberry ice cream. Which is why she went to the ball dressed as a chef.

Turn to page 119 to make the basic Adult Standing Hedgehog. Then make her chef's hat and apron as described below.

MATERIALS

20 x 45cm (8 x 18in) white medium-weight
   cotton-type fabric
Horizontally-striped blue/white medium-weight
   cotton-type fabric, 8cm (3in) deep x 11cm (4¼in) wide
50cm (½yd) white satin ribbon, 1.5mm (¹⁄₁₆in) wide, for hat
60cm (¾yd) matching blue satin or grosgrain ribbon,
   3mm (⅛in) wide, for apron
Matching threads
14 x 36cm (5½ x 14in) thin white card
Dry-stick adhesive
Clear adhesive

1. Following the diagrams on page 80, cut an 11cm (4¼in) diameter circle of card, and two strips of card 6cm (2¼in) deep x 24cm (9½in) wide. Then cut an 18cm (7in) diameter circle of white fabric, and a strip 10 x 26cm (3¾ x 10¼in). Mark the edge of the circle equally into eight.

2. Cut a 7cm (2¾in) diameter circle in a piece of waste card; roll up one of the card strips and put it into the hole, allowing it to open out inside so that it fits snugly against the sides. Mark the overlap, take the card out and glue the join to form a cylinder. Mark the top edge of the cylinder equally into eight.

3. Lightly glue the card circle to the wrong side of the fabric circle, centres matching. Then gather round the outer edge of the fabric. Fit this circle over the top of the cylinder, matching and pinning the marked points; draw up the gathers to fit, distributing them evenly, and stitch through the card.

4. Measure the second card strip around the first one and mark the point where they join (allowing for the gathered fabric); cut away the excess card. Glue the card lightly to the wrong side of the fabric strip, positioning as indicated by the broken line on the diagram; one short edge should be level with the edge of the fabric, and the fabric overlapping equally along the other three sides. Fold the surplus along the top edge over the card and glue to the back, but leave the overlap at the bottom free.

5. Glue the covered strip around the cylinder, lower edges of card level. Glue the fabric overlapping the join, then turn the surplus fabric at the bottom up and glue it neatly inside the hat.

6. Cut the white ribbon in half and stitch at each side for strings to tie in a bow under her chin, to keep the hat in place.

7. Cut the apron fabric along the thread to avoid having to make hems; use the selvedge for the lower edge, if possible.

Turn over 1cm (⅜in) at the top and herringbone-stitch over the raw edge to make a hem on the wrong side.

Thread blue ribbon through this channel and use it to tie the apron in position.

REDSKIN BIG CHIEF HEDGEHOG

When Barleycorn has finished reading his Wild West books, he shares them with Mr Hedgehog — who loves stories about the Redskins. He can't imagine anything more comfortable than hibernating in a wigwam with a glowing camp fire outside. He searched Blackberry Hollow for feathers, then borrowed all his wife's necklaces, to make his impressive outfit.

Turn to page 119 to make the basic Adult Standing Hedgehog. Then dress him as described below. If you haven't any feathers, cut them from coloured paper, drawing in the lines with a fine black pen.

MATERIALS

Coloured feathers or alternative (see above)
50cm (½yd) striped grosgrain ribbon, 23mm (1in) wide
2 scraps (or spots) of brown Velcro touch-and-close
fastening (or use snap fasteners)
Matching threads
Several strings of small coloured wooden beads
Clear adhesive

1. Cut the ribbon in half and, beginning at the centre, glue feathers along one piece, arranging them artistically to form the headdress (see the photograph); glue the *front* of the feathers to the ribbon, so that the backs are uppermost — curling towards you. Glue more, shorter, feathers on top, continuing until you are satisfied. Trim off any overlapping feathers along the lower edge.

2. Glue the other length of ribbon on top, folding the corners neatly under at each end to form a point.

Oversew the two lengths of ribbon neatly together along the lower edge.

3. Fit over the hedgehog's head and mark the position at each side for fixing. Stitch circles of Velcro, or snap fasteners, to the hedgehog and to the inside of the headdress ribbon at these points.

4. Remove the headdress and loop strings of beads across the hedgehog's front, as illustrated, catching them to the body just above and behind the paws. Then replace the headdress.

Grandma and Grandpa's Golden Wedding

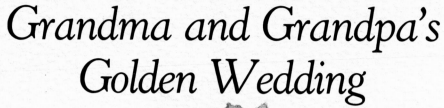

Flop came in and shut the front door. Autumn had arrived and it was getting colder. He could hear Flip talking on the telephone.

'That was Mr Speedwell,' Flip told him, putting down the receiver, 'Grandma and Grandpa Speedwell are celebrating their Golden Wedding, and the squirrels are giving a party.'

'Are we invited?' squeaked Flop, jumping up and down.

'Better than that,' grinned Flip, 'the family are giving them a very special present — and they are going to pay us to gift-wrap it for them!'

Once more the pixies put on their hats and chased off down Blackberry Lane in the hope of earning some money.

Flip had quite forgotten to ask what the present was. But when they saw it, the pixies were suddenly speechless with envy. The squirrels had bought Grandma and Grandpa Speedwell a beautiful new television set.

'Their old one was broken,' Filbert Speedwell explained. 'It can't be mended. They love watching television so much, so we've bought them a new one. It's colour too,' he smiled, 'the old one was only black and white.'

The pixies spent the whole morning wrapping and tying up the new television set. While they worked Flip was deep in thought. Flop kept very quiet because he could see Flip had something on his mind.

Eventually Flip said: 'I've had an idea.'

'I thought so,' nodded Flop.

'Let's ask them if we can have their old television set!' Flip said.

'But it's broken,' said Flop.

'Yes, I know,' agreed Flip, 'but we're never going to earn enough money to buy ourselves a new one. So a broken set would be better than nothing at all. At least we'll be able to tell the neighbours we've got television. And what's more,' he told Flop enthusiastically, 'if we stand in front of the screen, we'll be able to see ourselves.'

Flop thought this a brilliant idea, so together the pixies plucked up the courage to ask Filbert if they could have the old set as their payment for wrapping the present.

Filbert was delighted. 'It'll save me taking it to the rubbish dump,' he laughed, 'if you're sure you want a set that doesn't work.'

'Oh we do! We do!' shouted the pixies happily. 'Thank you, Sir!'

And laughing with excitement they pushed the old television set home in their wheelbarrow.

MR FILBERT SPEEDWELL

 ## Speedwell & Son — Family Grocers

He's taken the afternoon off to host his parents' Golden Wedding party, leaving his young assistant, Nutty Cobb, in charge of the village store.

Filbert Speedwell likes to wear casual, rather sporty, clothes when he's not in the shop. But if you are making the toy for a small child, omit his buttons and buckle.

First turn to page 105 to make the basic Adult Squirrel; then continue below.

MATERIALS
15 x 50cm (6 x 20in) medium-weight striped fabric for his trousers
25cm (10in) square lightweight patterned fabric (or handkerchief) for his scarf
30cm (12in) square red felt for his jacket
20cm (¼yd) woven braid, 20mm (¾in) wide, for his belt
Small (20mm/¾in) buckle for belt
2 small buttons for his jacket
18cm (7in) bias binding to match trousers
Matching threads
Clear adhesive

1. Cut the trousers twice in striped fabric, reversing the pattern to match the stripes. Open out both pieces and cut away the tail section at one corner only (reverse the second piece). (*Note*: if you prefer to make the trousers in felt, use the pattern for Stationmaster Speedwell's trousers, and follow those directions.)

2. Bind the raw curved edge of the tail section on each piece between d-e.

3. Join each piece between a-b. Then join the two pieces together between c-a-d, to form the centre front and back seams. Clip the curves.

4. Make a 1cm (⅜in) hem around the waist (herr-ingbone-stitch over the raw edge). Make similar hems around the lower edge of each leg. Turn to the right side.

5. Gather close to the top edge (between e-e), then fit trousers on squirrel and draw up round the waist, catching the back corners (e-e) securely together with a thread taken from side to side through the tail several times (use a darning needle to do this).

6. Fix the buckle in the middle of the braid, then pin the braid smoothly over the top edge of his trousers, buckle at centre front; stitch ends of braid securely to hold in position.

7. Cut the edges of the scarf along the straight of the fabric, then draw a few threads along each edge to prevent fraying. Fold in half diagonally and knot tightly round his neck, as illustrated.

8. Cut the jacket back once, and the front, sleeve and pocket twice each, in felt; note higher cutting lines on back and front for Filbert.

9. Oversew the front pieces to the back at each shoulder (h-j).
Gather the top edge of each sleeve between the circles. Fit the sleeves into the armholes, matching the side edges (k) and centre top to the shoulder seam (j). Draw up the gathers to fit and stitch into place.
Join the sleeve and side seams (l-k-m). Turn to the right side.
Stitch buttons to the jacket front, and glue a pocket at each side, as illustrated.

10. Fit the jacket on the squirrel and, if necessary, catch the lower corners together at the back by stitching through the tail as for the trousers.

MRS RUSSET
SPEEDWELL

Serving behind the counter in the village store gave Mrs Squirrel plenty of ideas for the party she and her husband were giving to celebrate his parents' Golden Wedding anniversary. Along with a plentiful supply of assorted nuts, she'd hoarded all kinds of goodies packed in tins and boxes and cardboard cartons.

Russet made herself a very smart dress for the party, colour-matching her necklace to match the flowered fabric. But omit the beads if the toy is for a small child.

MATERIALS

25cm (¼yd) short reddish-brown fur fabric, 90cm (36in) wide
Long reddish-brown fur fabric, 22cm (8½in) deep x 30cm (12in) wide, for the tail
25 x 60cm (10 x 24in) firmly woven medium-weight cotton-type dress fabric (see basic Adult Rabbit)
6.5 x 12.5cm (2½ x 5in) brown felt (to tone with fur)
5cm (2in) square black felt
60cm (¾yd) lace, 10mm (⅜in) deep, to trim hem
50cm (⅝yd) single-face satin ribbon (to tone), 9mm (⅜in) wide
3 short strings of small wooden beads in toning colours
Polyester stuffing
Matching and black (optional) threads
Scraps of stiff card or plastic (double cereal carton or cottage cheese tub lid)
Clear adhesive

1. Use the pattern pieces for the Adult Squirrel (pages 106-7). In short brown fur fabric, cut the head gusset once; cut the leg and the face twice each (reversing the pattern to cut the second face); cut the ear and the paw four times each. In the dress fabric, cut the skirt 14 x 60cm (5½ x 24in); then cut the body and the sleeve twice each. Cut the tail twice (reversing the second

piece) in the long brown fur. Cut the sole twice in felt; then cut it again slightly smaller, following the broken line, in card or stiff plastic. Mark notches.

2. Turn to page 105 and follow the directions for the basic Adult Squirrel but, when you reach step 5, make the 'sleeve-and-paw' version of the basic Adult Rabbit (page 100) using dress fabric.

3. Join the two short edges of the skirt for the centre back seam but for 6cm (2½in) only, leaving 8cm (3in) open above; turn under and hem each side of the opening. Press, then turn to the right side.

4. Mark the top edge into four. Then turn under a narrow hem and gather close to the fold. Fit on the squirrel and pin to the figure just above the bodice/legs seam, with the marked points at sides (level with body seams) and the centre front; pin the back corners close against the tail. Draw up the gathers to fit, distributing them evenly between the pins, and stitch securely into position, using double thread and a long darning needle.

5. Turn up the hem to the required length and stitch. Then stitch lace to the wrong side, so that about 5mm (¼in) is visible beneath the lower edge.

6. Fix a band of ribbon round her waist, catching the ends securely at each side of the tail.

7. Fix a band of ribbon round each wrist, over the edge of the sleeve; overlap the ends, then turn the top cut end under and stitch neatly.

8. Fix the beads around her neck, catching at the back to hold in position.

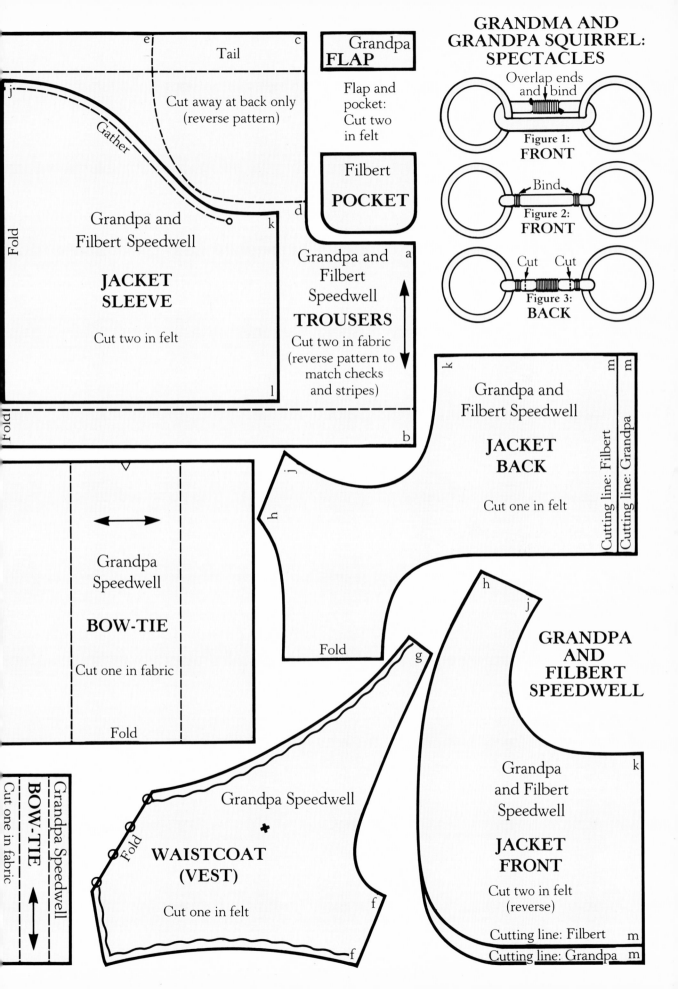

Tail

e

c

Grandpa
FLAP

Flap and
pocket:
Cut two
in felt

GRANDMA AND
GRANDPA SQUIRREL:
SPECTACLES

Overlap ends
and bind

Figure 1:
FRONT

j

Cut away at back only
(reverse pattern)

Gather

Filbert
POCKET

Bind

Figure 2:
FRONT

d

Grandpa and
Filbert Speedwell

JACKET
SLEEVE

Cut two in felt

k

Grandpa and
Filbert
Speedwell

TROUSERS

Cut two in fabric
(reverse pattern to
match checks
and stripes)

a

Cut   Cut

Figure 3:
BACK

Fold

l

b

k

m   m

Fold

Grandpa and
Filbert Speedwell

JACKET
BACK

Cut one in felt

Cutting line: Filbert

Cutting line: Grandpa

j

h

Grandpa
Speedwell

BOW-TIE

Cut one in fabric

Fold

Fold

h

j

g

GRANDPA
AND
FILBERT
SPEEDWELL

Grandpa Speedwell

BOW-TIE

Cut one in fabric

Grandpa Speedwell

Grandpa Speedwell

Fold

WAISTCOAT
(VEST)

Cut one in felt

f

f

Grandpa
and Filbert
Speedwell

JACKET
FRONT

Cut two in felt
(reverse)

k

Cutting line: Filbert   m

Cutting line: Grandpa   m

GRANDPA SPEEDWELL

Old Mr Speedwell had hoped both his sons would go into the family firm. But Acorn was always mad about trains, so his father didn't try to stop him when he got a job with the railway. Now that Acorn has been made stationmaster at Blackberry Halt, he couldn't be more proud. And when the time came for him to retire, his younger son Filbert had a very capable wife, so Mr Speedwell knew that the village store would be in good paws.

Grandpa Speedwell makes a lovely mascot for anyone of any age. But if you are making him as a toy for a small child, omit the beads, buttons, spectacles and watch-chain.

First turn to page 105 to make the basic Adult Squirrel; then continue below.

MATERIALS

15 x 50cm (6 x 20in) medium-weight olive checked fabric for his trousers
14 x 16cm (5½ x 6¼in) honey felt for his waistcoat (vest)
30cm (12in) square dark grey felt for jacket
10 x 20cm (4 x 8in) medium-weight olive spotted fabric for bow-tie
50cm (⅝yd) narrow olive braid, about 6-8mm (¼in) wide, for waistcoat
3 small buttons for jacket
4 small wooden beads for waistcoat (vest)
12cm (5in) string of tiny gold beads for watch-chain
2 gilt curtain rings, 2cm (¾in) diameter, for spectacles
6cm (2½in) gold-covered narrow round elastic (or gold cord or wire), for spectacles
20cm (¼yd) narrow round elastic for bow-tie
18cm (7in) bias binding to match trousers
Matching threads
Clear adhesive

1. Follow the directions for Filbert Speedwell's trousers, steps 1-5 (page 89), matching the check pattern in the same way.

2. Cut the waistcoat (vest) in honey felt. Glue braid along the upper and lower edges, as indicated by the wavy line.

Stitch wooden bead 'buttons' at (o)s. Stitch the ends of the gold beads at (x)s to hang across the front between the third and fourth buttons, as illustrated, for his watch-chain.

Place the waistcoat flat on his chest, taking the side edges (f-f) smoothly round and pinning them over the side seams of the body. Take the top points (g) over the shoulders and around the neck, pinning to the body just behind the head. Make sure the waistcoat fits very snugly, then stitch the sides and top piece to the body, removing the pins.

3. Cut the two pieces for the bow-tie once each in fabric. Fold the larger piece in half lengthways and join the two long edges. Turn to the right side, folding as the broken lines, so that the seam is level with the notches; tack.

With the seam at the back, make a formal bow (Trimmings: page 7), binding it with the smaller piece of fabric folded lengthways into three, raw edges underneath, as broken lines on pattern.

Fix to the centre of the elastic, then knot the ends at the back of the neck.

4. Cut the jacket back once, and the front, sleeve and pocket flap twice each, in grey felt.

Follow the directions for Filbert Speedwell's jacket, steps 9 and 10 (page 89), gluing on the flaps instead of pockets.

5. To make his spectacles, loop a 5.5cm (2¼in) length of elastic (or alternative) through the curtain rings; overlap the ends at the back as figure 1, and bind with thread (don't bother to make a neat join).

Now bind the elastic tightly close against each ring — as neatly as possible this time — as in figure 2. Then cut away the centre section of elastic at the back, a fraction away from the bound area at each side (figure 3).

Place the elastic bridge over the top of the nose and stitch the rings at each side of the nose, above and below the point where the elastic joins the ring.

GRANDMA SPEEDWELL

Neat and tidy in her blouse and skirt with the practical apron she has always worn, and a warm shawl round her shoulders, old Mrs Speedwell sighs with satisfaction when she sees how well her younger son has done. A pretty but sensible wife, who works just as hard as he does in the shop, and two charming grandchildren; what more could a proud grandmother want!

If the toy is for a small child, omit spectacles.

MATERIALS
25cm (¼yd) short reddish-brown fur fabric, 90cm (36in) wide
Long reddish-brown fur fabric, 22cm (8½in) deep x 30cm (12in) wide, for the tail
10 x 60cm (4 x 24in) firmly woven medium-weight cotton-type fabric for her blouse (see basic Adult Rabbit)
14 x 60cm (5½ x 24in) medium-weight cotton-type fabric for her skirt
10 x 15cm (4 x 6in) cream medium-weight fabric for her apron
25cm (10in) square lightweight plaid or check fabric (or handkerchief) for her shawl
6.5 x 12.5cm (2½ x 5in) brown felt (to tone with fur)
5cm (2in) square black felt
1m (1¼yd) cream lace, 10mm (⅜in) deep
50cm (⅝yd) dark narrow lace to edge shawl
2 gilt curtain rings, 2cm (¾in) diameter, for spectacles
6cm (2½in) gold-covered narrow round elastic (or gold cord or wire), for spectacles
Polyester stuffing
Matching and black (optional) sewing threads
Scraps of stiff card or plastic (double cereal carton or cottage cheese tub lid)
Clear adhesive

1. Use the pattern pieces for the basic Adult Squirrel (pages 106-7). In short brown fur fabric, cut the head gusset once; cut the leg and the face twice each (reversing the pattern to cut the second face); cut the ear and the paw four times each. In the blouse fabric, cut the body and the sleeve twice each. Cut the tail twice (reversing the second piece) in the long brown fur. Cut the sole twice in felt; then cut it again slightly smaller, following the broken line, in card or stiff plastic. Mark notches.

2. Turn to page 105 and follow the directions for the basic Adult Squirrel, but when you reach step 5, make the 'sleeve-and-paw' version of the basic Adult Rabbit, using the blouse fabric. *Note*: when you have turned up the lower edge of the sleeve, but before you gather it (step 11b), tack lace so that the straight edge covers about 3mm (⅛in) fabric, and the remainder overlaps below; gather the lace and fabric together, to form a frill round her wrist.

3. Join the two short edges of the skirt fabric for the centre back seam, but for 6cm (2½in) only, leaving 8cm (3in) open above; fold edges of opening down and hem. Press, then turn to the right side.

4. Mark the top edge into four. Then turn under a narrow hem and gather close to the fold. Fit on the squirrel and pin to the figure just above the blouse/legs seam, with the marked points at sides (level with body seams) and the centre front; pin the back corners close against the tail. Draw up the gathers to fit, distributing them evenly between the pins, and stitch securely into position, using double thread and a long darning needle.

5. Turn up the hem to the required length and stitch.

6. Turn under and stitch a narrow hem down each side of the apron fabric. Stitch lace over the raw lower edge. Turn the top edge under and gather close to the fold; draw up to measure 8cm (3in). Pin over skirt, centres matching and top edges level; stitch into place.

7. Gather the remaining lace and draw up round the neck, join at back. Distribute the gathers evenly to form a frilly collar.

8. Fold the shawl fabric diagonally in half; stitch trimming along the two top raw edges only.

Drape round her shoulders (tucking down behind the tail) and catch the front corners over the waist as illustrated.

9. Make and fit her spectacles as directed for Grandpa Speedwell (page 90 — step 5).

SKIPPY

SPEEDWELL

Her mother has taught her how to cook, and her favourite job is baking gingerbread men to sell in the shop. Skippy says that one day she will have her own bakery and be famous for her blackberry buns.

The smaller squirrels are made in exactly the same way as the grown-ups, so the list of materials below includes cream fur for her chest. But if you are dressing Skippy as illustrated, the cream fur will be covered, so if you haven't any, just cut the body twice in brown fur instead.

MATERIALS

15 x 75cm (6 x 30in) short reddish-brown fur fabric, for the body

Cream fur fabric, 7cm (3in) deep x 10cm (4in) wide, for the chest (optional — see above)

Long reddish-brown fur fabric, 15cm (6in) deep x 22cm (9in) wide, for the tail

5 x 10cm (2 x 5in) brown felt (to tone with fur)

4cm (1½in) square black felt

Polyester stuffing

Matching and black (optional) threads

Scraps of stiff card or plastic (double cereal carton or cottage cheese tub lid)

Clear adhesive

10 x 40cm (4 x 15in) medium-weight cotton-type dark flowered fabric for her dress

30cm (12in) white broderie anglaise (eyelet embroidery), 25-30mm (1-1¼in) deep, for collar

40cm (15in) coloured broderie anglaise (eyelet embroidery) or lace, 15mm (½in) deep, to trim hem of dress

25cm (10in) bias binding to match dress

30cm (12in) white bias binding for collar

40cm (½yd) white satin ribbon, 1.5mm (¹⁄₁₆in) wide (or 25cm (10in) narrow round elastic) for collar

20cm (¼yd) single-face blue satin ribbon, 39mm (1½in) wide, for bow

15cm (6in) narrow round elastic

Matching threads

1. *Using the pattern pieces for the Junior Squirrel* (page 108), follow the directions for the 'all-fur' version of the basic Adult Squirrel (page 105).

2. Cut the dress pattern once in fabric.

3. Bind the armhole edges, stretching the binding as you do so.

4. Join the centre back seam above the notch. Turn under the raw edges below the notch and hem.

5. Turn under the top edge along the broken line, turn the raw edge narrowly under and stitch.

6. Turn up a 1cm (⅜in) hem along the lower edge and stitch. Then stitch trimming so that it protrudes just below the hem.

7. Thread elastic through the top channels; fit dress on the squirrel and draw up elastic round the neck. Catch the lower corners together at the back with a thread taken from side to side through the tail several times (use a darning needle to do this).

8. Bind the top edge of the white broderie anglaise. Then thread ribbon through the binding and draw up round the neck, tying in a bow at the back. (Elastic may be used instead of ribbon if preferred.)

9. Make a formal bow (Trimmings: page 7) from 15cm (6in) blue ribbon, bound with 4cm (2in). Stitch to the top of her head as illustrated.

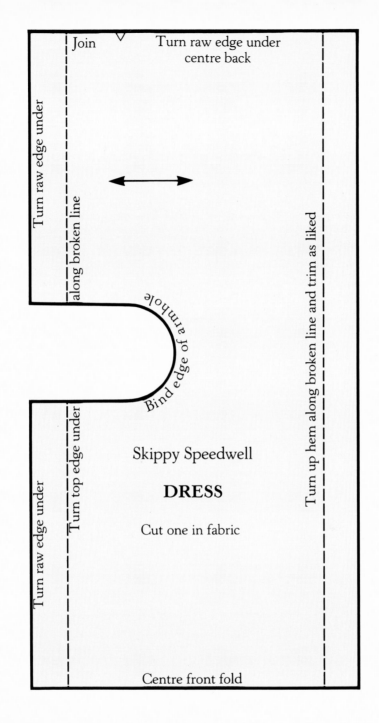

Join

Turn raw edge under
centre back

Turn raw edge under

along broken line

Bind edge of armhole

Turn top edge under

Turn raw edge under

Turn up hem along broken line and trim as liked

Skippy Speedwell

DRESS

Cut one in fabric

Centre front fold

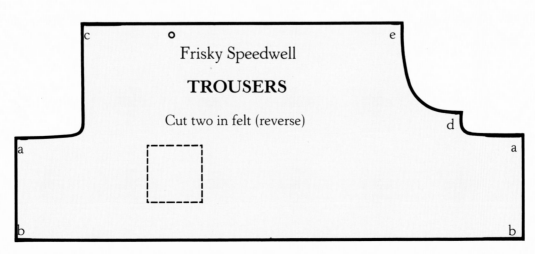

c   o   e

Frisky Speedwell

TROUSERS

Cut two in felt (reverse)

d

a   a

b   b

FRISKY

SPEEDWELL

Frisky Speedwell just loves to help his parents in the village shop — when he isn't listening to the tales his grandpa tells about the old days in Blackberry Hollow.

MATERIALS
15 x 55cm (6 x 24in) short reddish-brown fur fabric, for the body
Long reddish-brown fur fabric, 15cm (6in) deep x 22cm (9in) wide, for the tail
10 x 30cm (4 x 12in) firmly woven medium-weight cotton-type fabric for his shirt (see basic Adult Rabbit)
5 x 10cm (2 x 5in) brown felt (to tone with fur)
4cm (1½in) square black felt
15cm (6in) square felt for his trousers
Scrap of felt or fabric for patches
Polyester stuffing
Matching and black (optional) threads
Scraps of stiff card or plastic (double cereal carton or cottage cheese tub lid)
Clear adhesive

1. Use the pattern pieces for the Junior Squirrel (page 108). In short brown fur fabric, cut the head gusset once; cut the leg and the face twice each (reversing the pattern to cut the second face); cut the ear and the paw four times each. In the shirt fabric, cut the body and the sleeve twice each. Cut the tail twice (reversing the second piece) in the long brown fur. Cut the sole twice

in felt; then cut it again slightly smaller, following the broken line, in card or stiff plastic. Mark notches.

2. Turn to page 105 and follow the directions for the basic Adult Squirrel, but when you reach step 5, make the 'sleeve-and-paw' version of the basic Adult Rabbit, using your shirt fabric.

3. In felt, cut the trousers twice, and two straps, about 6mm (¼in) wide x 10cm (4in) long.

4. Oversew each leg together between a-b. Then join the two pieces between c-a-d, to form the centre front and back seams. Turn to the right side.

5. Cut patches about 15mm (⅝in) square, and appliqué or glue to each knee.

6. Glue one end of each strap behind the top edge of the trousers at (o)s.

7. Gather the waist edge.

8. Fit trousers on the squirrel and draw up round waist, catching the back corners (e) securely together with a thread taken from side to side through the tail several times (use a darning needle to do this). Take the straps over the shoulders and glue them to the back corners of the trousers (e); trim off surplus.

The Little Ones' Christmas Party

Christmas was coming, and Blackberry Hollow was preparing for the festivities. Tiny coloured lights were twinkling in the windows, the carol singers were practising, and Christmas puddings were being stirred.

'Let's give a party,' suggested Flip. 'We could make sausage rolls and mince pies and toffee apples — and have a Christmas tree . . .'

'And play musical toadstools and hide-and-seek,' broke in Flop.

'We'll invite all the little ones,' continued Flip, 'and ask Grandpa Speedwell to dress up as Santa Claus.'

The pixies worked very hard preparing for their party. For a whole week their kitchen was full of wonderful smells, and at the end it was bursting with tempting things to eat. They cut down a tree and brought it home on their wheelbarrow, then they decorated it with shiny baubles and tinsel. Old Mr Speedwell said he'd be happy to play Santa Claus, so they made him a red suit and a long white beard.

On Christmas Eve Flip and Flop welcomed the little animals as they trooped into Toadstool Cottage, giggling with anticipation.

Grandpa Speedwell made a wonderful Santa Claus, and the pixies thanked him very much. 'And thank you for the television set, too,' added Flip.

'Are you still happy with it?' asked Grandpa a little doubtfully.

'Oh yes! replied Flip emphatically.

'There's only one problem,' confided Flop, 'it isn't high enough to see ourselves on the screen, so we have to lie on the floor.'

Grandpa looked puzzled. 'Why not put it on the table?' he asked.

'Because we wouldn't have anywhere to eat our supper,' they explained.

Grandpa gazed round the room. 'What about that great big book,' he said, pointing at Harriet Hemlock's Book of Spells, 'do you use it often?'

'Never!' replied the two pixies dismally.

'Well, stand it on that,' suggested Grandpa, and helped them lift it up.

Barnabas Brown noticed what they were doing. 'A television set!' he shouted excitedly, and rushed over to turn the knobs.

'It's no good doing that,' Flip told him, 'it doesn't work.'

'But it does,' said Barnabas.

And sure enough, when it was standing on the Book of Spells — the broken television set worked perfectly.

'But it's a black and white set,' gasped Grandpa Speedwell, 'and your picture is in colour.'

'So Harriet Hemlock really was a witch after all!' laughed Flop.

And Flip had to agree.

SANTA CLAUS

Grandpa Speedwell

The success of the pixies' party owed much to the presence of Grandpa Speedwell — heavily disguised as Santa Claus. None of the little ones guessed it wasn't the real Father Christmas; even his bushy tail didn't give him away!

Turn to page 105 to make the basic Adult Squirrel, adding spectacles (if required) as directed for Grandpa Speedwell (page 90 — step 5). Then dress him as described below.

If you are in a hurry it is possible to buy lambswool trimming by the metre (yard). But the method described below works very well and is easy to do. Choose a fairly short fur and, if possible, cut the strips lengthways, along the knitted lines. However, if you are buying the fur specially, purchase only the amount you will need (as shown below), and cut the strips across the fabric.

MATERIALS

30cm (12in) red felt, 70cm (27in) wide, for his tunic, breeches and cap
17 x 20cm (6½ x 8in) black felt for boots
12 x 70cm (4½ x 28in) or 40 x 19cm (16 x 7½in) white fur fabric (see above)
30cm (12in) black grosgrain ribbon, 20mm (¾in) wide, for his belt
Small (20mm/¾in) buckle for belt
Large white pompon or white knitting yarn
Cotton wool (absorbent cotton)
Matching threads
Clear adhesive

1. Use the patterns, and follow the directions, for Filbert the Pirate's breeches and boots in the previous chapter (page 69); cut the breeches in red felt and the boots and soles in black.

2. For his tunic, use the patterns for the back and sleeve of the Pirate's jacket (pages 70-1), noting the higher cutting line on the back. The front is on page 99. Follow figure 1 to make a pattern for his cap.

Cut the tunic front and sleeve twice each in red felt, and the back and cap once each.

3. Oversew the front pieces of the tunic to the back at each shoulder (h-j).

Gather the top edge of each sleeve between the circles. Fit the sleeves into the armholes, matching the side edges (k) and centre top to the shoulder seam (j). Draw up the gathers to fit and stitch into place.

Join the sleeve and side seams (l-k-m). Turn to the right side.

4. Cut two strips of fur fabric, each 4cm (1½in) wide x 15cm (6in) long, for his cuffs. Fold each in half lengthways and oversew the long edges together, making long stitches and taking up only a fraction of the fabric (figure 2a). Now flatten the strip, so that the join falls in the centre (figure 2b); stitch back along the join, making long running stitches that take up just enough fabric to catch the front and back together (figure 2c). Right side outside, join the short edges to form a circle; fit over the lower edge of the sleeve and catch into position from inside the sleeve.

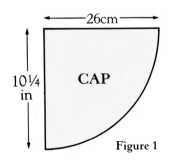

Figure 1

SANTA SPEEDWELL

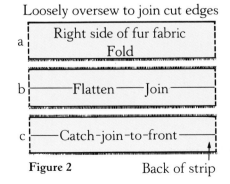

Figure 2   Back of strip

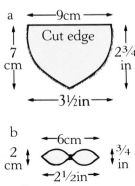

Figure 3

5. Fit the tunic on the squirrel; overlap and pin the centre front edges, then stitch neatly.

6. Cut a strip of fur fabric 4cm (1½in) wide x 25cm (10in) long for his collar. Prepare it as described for the cuffs, then fit round his neck, joining at the back. Prepare a similar strip, 33cm (13in) long and pin it round the lower edge of his tunic, beginning and ending at the back; catch into place from inside the tunic. Catch the back corners of the tunic together through the tail.

7. Fix the buckle at the centre of the ribbon, then fix round his waist, catching the ends at the back alongside his tail.

8. Cut two circles of black felt for buttons and glue at the centre front, above and below his belt.

9. Oversew the straight edges of the cap together to form a cone. Turn to the right side.

Cut a strip of fur fabric 7cm (2¾in) wide x 40cm (15¾in) long. Join the short edges to form a circle. Pin the strip round the bottom of the cap, right sides together and cut edges level, then oversew the lower edges together. Pull the strip down, then fold it in half, taking the other cut edge up inside and stitching it to the lower edge of the cap.

10. Stitch pompon to point of cap (see page 9) if making your own). Fit the cap on the squirrel and bring the point over as illustrated; pin it into position, then remove the cap and catch into place from inside.

11. Cut and tear a piece of cotton wool (absorbent cotton) into shape for his beard, roughly following figure 3a. Bind a separate piece tightly at the centre and twist the ends between your fingertips to form points, as figure 3b. Then stitch the moustache at the centre of the cut edge of the beard. Catch beard and moustache lightly to his face, as illustrated.

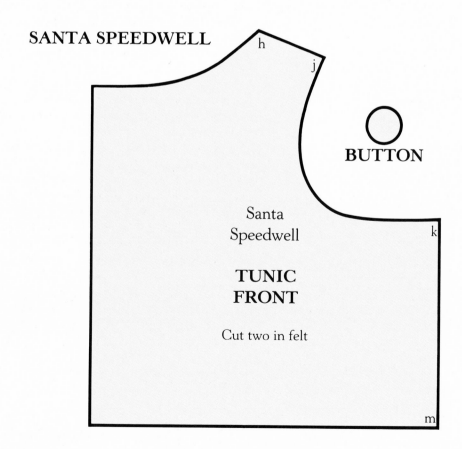

SANTA SPEEDWELL

h

j

BUTTON

Santa
Speedwell

TUNIC
FRONT

Cut two in felt

k

m

THE BASIC TOYS

ADULT RABBIT

This is the basic pattern for a grown-up rabbit. There are two versions. In the first, the whole toy is made from fur fabric in one or more colours; in the second version, the head, paws and lower part of the body are all made from fur, but the upper part of the body and the arms are fabric, forming his shirt, or her bodice or blouse. Choose a firmly woven, medium-weight fabric for this; thin fabrics are unsatisfactory when joined to the thick fur fabric, and are not firm enough to be stuffed.

For the 'all-fur' version use the arm pattern; for a shirt, blouse or bodice, you will need the sleeve-and-paw patterns instead.

Look for a fur fabric with a fairly short, thick, pile. The animals are quite small, and a longer fur would be out of proportion. If you feel the fur is a little too long around the features or on the paws, trim it away — but go very carefully; you can always take more off . . . but you can't put it back!

MATERIALS
See the individual directions for the specific rabbit you are
    planning to make

SEAM ALLOWANCES
5mm (³/₁₆in) for the Adult — slightly less for the Junior
    version

1. Cut out your pieces as directed in step 1 of the directions for the character you are making.

2. Mark the eye accurately on each face piece.

For a smiling rabbit, mark the mouth very carefully on both face pieces. To do this, stick a pin straight down through the pattern and fabric every 3mm (⅛in) or so; push the heads right down against the paper, then gently ease the pattern away to leave the pins stuck in the fabric. Using black sewing thread, back-stitch along this line, following the position of the pins very accurately and removing them as you sew (make sure your stitches show clearly on the right side).

3. Join the two face pieces between A-B, making sure the two mouth lines meet exactly. Using three strands

of embroidery cotton, embroider over the mouth on the right side in stem (outline) stitch.

Cut the eyes in black felt (see Creating Character — cutting circles: page 7). Push a pin through the marked point on each side of the face, then push back the fur all round it and place the felt eye centrally on the point of the pin; push it down into position and appliqué (or glue) it into position.

4. Carefully match the tip of the gusset (a) to the top of the seam, then join it to each side of the face between a and the single notch. It is very important to do this accurately. Before *each stitch* match the raw edges of the face and gusset, taking care not to stretch either piece of fabric, remember that, as long as the edges are exactly together and the width of the seam is correct and even, you can't go wrong.

Then join the other end of each seam, between c and the double notch. Now gather each side of the gusset between the single and double notches. Pin the gusset to the face at each side, drawing up the gathers as you do so, and distributing them evenly along the length of the seam, easing the gusset in to fit round the top of the face. Stitch securely over the gathers. Turn to the right side.

5. Stuff the head quite firmly, pushing the filling well up into the nose and chin. Using a double thread, gather round the lower edge of the head, then draw up tightly and secure, leaving just a small hole no more than 2cm (¾in) in diameter (before securing your thread, check that the head is sufficiently stuffed, adding a little more filling under the chin).

6. Join each leg between d-e. Then join the two leg pieces between f-d-f, to form the centre front and back seams; the easiest way to do this is to begin at point d and join one side, then return to point d to join the other. Pin a sole to the lower edge of each leg, matching notches; *oversew* together.

7. Join the two body pieces together all round the curved edge, leaving the straight lower edge open.

8. Pin the lower edge of one side of the body (the front)

to the top edge of the legs, matching sides and centres. Stitch together, extending your stitching line at each end so that the back of the body is joined to the back of the legs for about 2cm (¾in) at each side, leaving a section open across the centre; turn under and tack the raw edges of the opening. Turn to the right side.

9. Push the inner soles down into the feet, holding temporarily in place with pins from the outside. Stuff the legs and the body firmly. Then pin the edges of the opening together, matching the centres. Stitch one half, then add some more filling to ensure the body is adequately stuffed at the centre; complete stitching.

10. Using a darning needle and double thread, take a stitch through the centre top of the body, from back to front, under the seam. Then take a stitch across the hole under the head, from front to back; and then repeat the first stitch through the body. Draw up, so that the head is in the correct position, then repeat the previous stitches to hold it in place. Now ladder stitch all round, alternately taking one stitch through the head and one through the body, securing them firmly together. The best way to do this is to go round once, taking quite large stitches; then, when you have checked everything looks right, go round again, taking smaller stitches and drawing your thread fairly taut.

11a. If you are making the 'all-fur' version, join two arm pieces all round, leaving the top edge open. Turn to the right side and stuff firmly, then gather all round the top edge and draw up tightly, leaving a small hole in the centre, and secure your thread.
11b. If you are making the 'sleeve-and-paw' version, join two paw pieces all round, leaving the straight top edge open. Turn to the right side and stuff firmly.
   Join the side seam of each sleeve (h-j) as far as the circle. Then turn under a narrow hem round the lower edge and gather close to the fold. Turn to the right side. Fit the paw inside, matching side seams to notches, and pin the edge of the sleeve to the paw as indicated by the broken line on the pattern; measure to make sure the paw extends exactly the right amount. Draw up the gathers evenly to fit and stitch together. Turn under a narrow hem all round the top edge of the sleeve and gather close to the fold. Then draw up tightly leaving a tiny hole in the centre, and secure your thread.

12. Using double thread, stitch the arms securely to the sides of the body, at shoulder level, over the seam, first catching the gathered centre of the arm over the seam, to position it, as you did the head.

13. To make each ear, *oversew* two pieces together all round, leaving the straight lower edge open. (*Don't* start at one corner and end at the other. Begin each side at the bottom corner and finish at the top, then you will find you can tuck the fur in neatly as you sew.) Turn to the right side.

14. Pin the ears halfway down the back of the head, the outer edges a fraction inside the edge of the gusset. Check the position, then stitch securely into place with a darning needle — across the raw edges at the bottom and up each side to the notch.

15. Cut the nose in black felt and glue into position over point a where the gusset joins the two face pieces. pieces.

16. If your rabbit requires a tail and you haven't a purchased pompon, make one from fluffy knitting yarn (see Trimmings: page 9). Stitch or glue it into position.

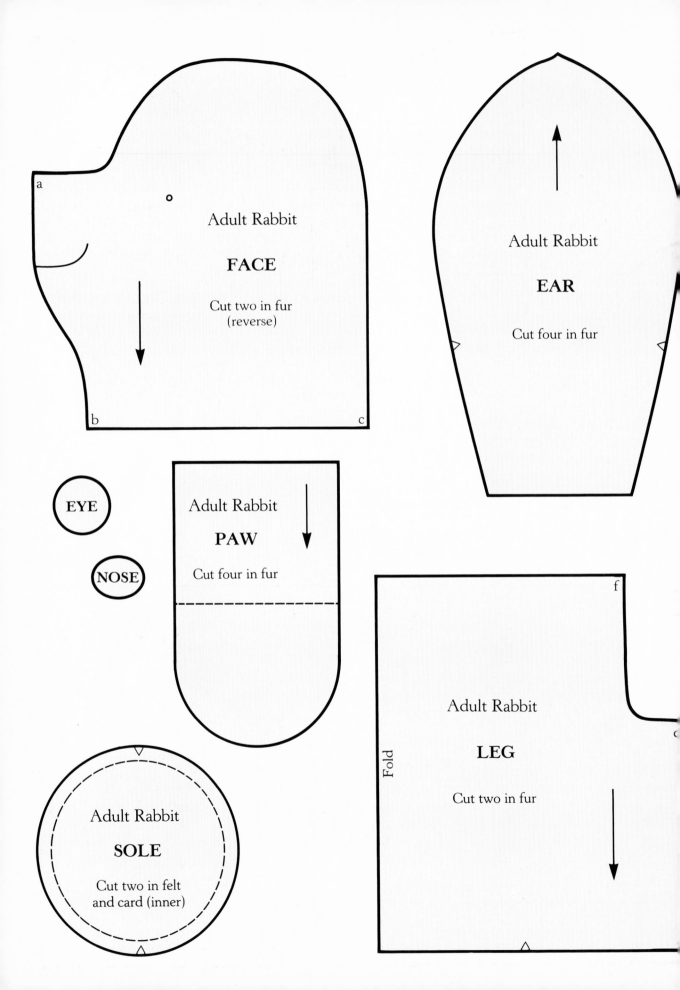

a

o

Adult Rabbit

FACE

Cut two in fur
(reverse)

b   c

Adult Rabbit

EAR

Cut four in fur

EYE

Adult Rabbit

PAW

Cut four in fur

NOSE

f

Fold

Adult Rabbit

LEG

Cut two in fur

Adult Rabbit

SOLE

Cut two in felt
and card (inner)

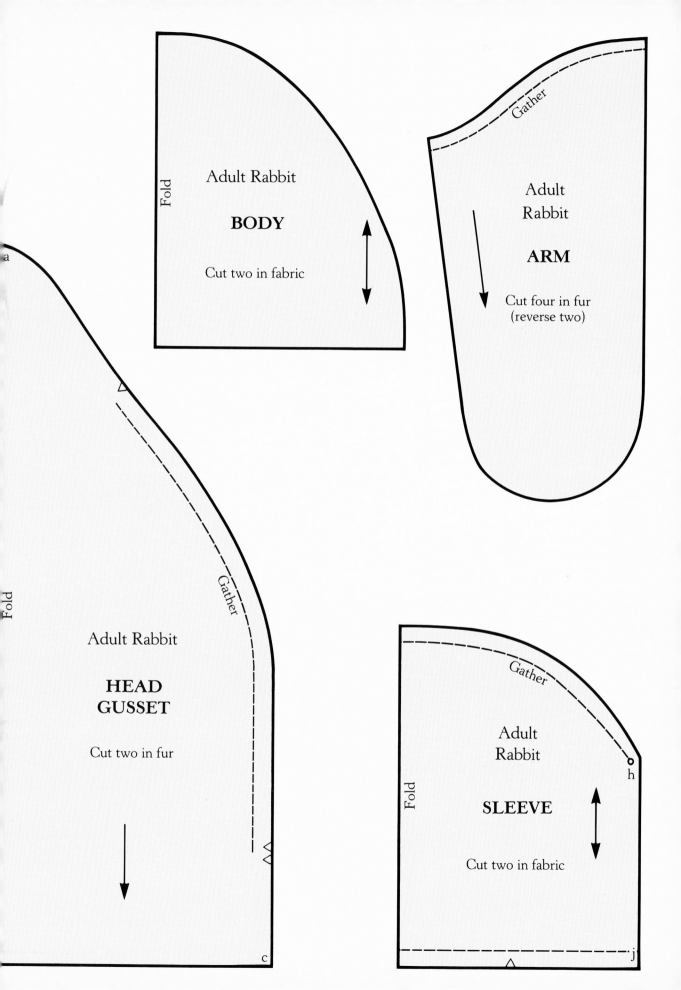

Fold

Adult Rabbit

BODY

Cut two in fabric

Gather

Adult Rabbit

ARM

Cut four in fur
(reverse two)

a

Fold

Gather

Adult Rabbit

HEAD GUSSET

Cut two in fur

c

Gather

h

Fold

Adult Rabbit

SLEEVE

Cut two in fabric

j

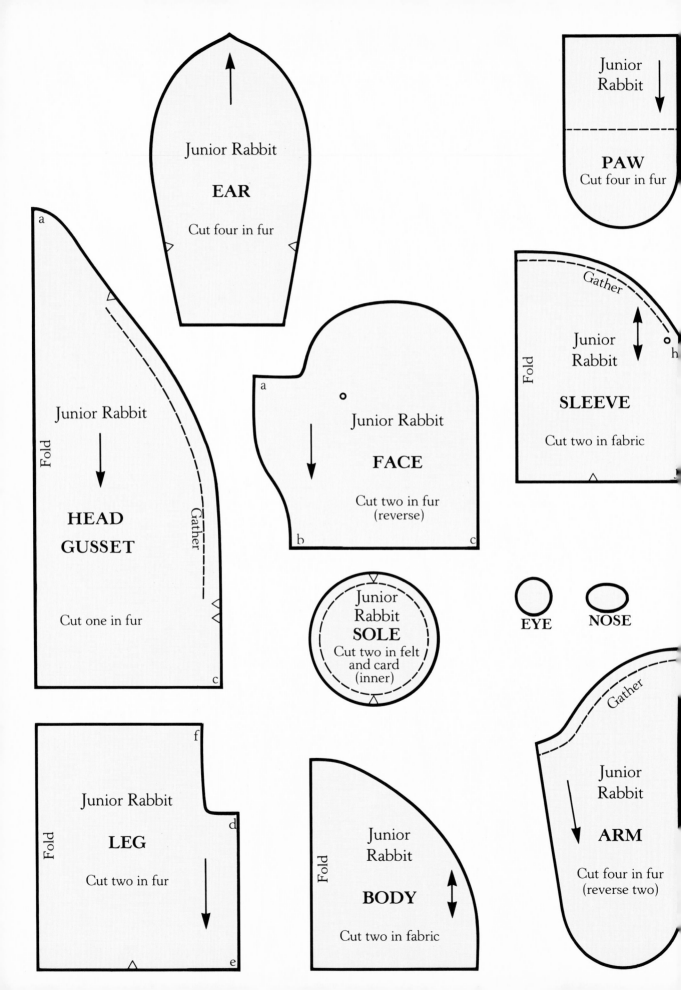

Junior Rabbit

EAR

Cut four in fur

Junior
Rabbit

PAW

Cut four in fur

Fold

Gather

Junior
Rabbit

SLEEVE

Cut two in fabric

a

Fold

Junior Rabbit

Gather

**HEAD
GUSSET**

Cut one in fur

c

a

Junior Rabbit

FACE

Cut two in fur
(reverse)

b   c

Junior
Rabbit
SOLE
Cut two in felt
and card
(inner)

EYE   **NOSE**

f

Junior Rabbit

Fold

LEG

Cut two in fur

d

e

Fold

Junior
Rabbit

BODY

Cut two in fabric

Gather

Junior
Rabbit

ARM

Cut four in fur
(reverse two)

ADULT SQUIRREL

The squirrel is very similar to the rabbit, and is made in much the same way. He has a furry body and arms, with a handsome cream chest. Of course the big difference is his bushy tail; try to find a thick, long fur for this, to contrast with the shorter fur you use for the body.

MATERIALS
25cm (¼yd) short reddish-brown fur fabric, 90cm (36in) wide, for the body
Cream fur fabric, 10cm (4in) deep x 15cm (6in) wide, for the chest
Long reddish-brown fur fabric, 22cm (8½in) deep x 30cm (12in) wide, for the tail
6.5 x 12.5cm (2½ x 5in) brown felt (to tone with fur)
5cm (2in) square black felt
Polyester stuffing
Stranded black embroidery cotton (optional)
Matching and black (optional) sewing threads
Scraps of stiff card or plastic (double cereal carton or cottage cheese tub lid)
Clear adhesive

SEAM ALLOWANCES
5mm (³⁄₁₆in) for the Adult — slightly less for the Junior version

1. In short brown fur fabric, cut the head gusset and the body once; cut the leg and the face twice each (reversing the pattern to cut the second face); cut the ear and the arm four times each (reversing two arm pieces). Cut the body once more in cream fur. Cut the tail twice (reversing the second piece) in the long brown fur. Cut the sole twice in felt; then cut it again slightly smaller, following the broken line, in card or stiff plastic. Mark notches.

2. Mark the eye accurately on each face piece.

3. Join the two face pieces between a-b.

4. Cut the eyes in black felt (see Creating Character —

cutting circles: page 7). If you prefer, the eyes may be glued on at the end. But if you wish to do them now, push a pin through the marked point on each side of the face, then push back the fur all round it and place the felt eye centrally on the point of the pin; push it down into position, making sure the points follow the direction of the arrows and are equally balanced. Appliqué (or glue) into position.

5. Now turn to the basic Adult Rabbit (page 100) and follow the directions for the 'all-fur' version: steps 4-13.

6. Pin the ears to each side of the head, overlapping the gusset seam (see the photographs for guidance); stitch securely into place around the bottom and up each side to the circle.

7. Oversew the tail pieces together all round, leaving the straight edge open; be sure to tuck all the long fur down between the seam, through to the outside. Stuff fully, but not firmly, then separate the straight edges and pin each to the back of the body, positioning the tail so that the lowest point is level with the bottom of the legs (so that the toy balances on the tail as well as the feet when it is standing). Ladder stitch the tail securely into place.

8. Cut the nose in black felt and glue into position over point a where the gusset joins the two face pieces. Glue the eyes on now if you have not already done so.

9. If you want your squirrel to have a mouth, make a single stitch, about 1cm (³⁄₈in) long, using six strands of black embroidery cotton, about 1cm (³⁄₈in) below the nose.

JUNIOR RABBITS AND SQUIRRELS

The younger animals are just smaller versions of the adults. Use the same type of fur fabric, but you may need to do a little more trimming round the paws when they are finished.

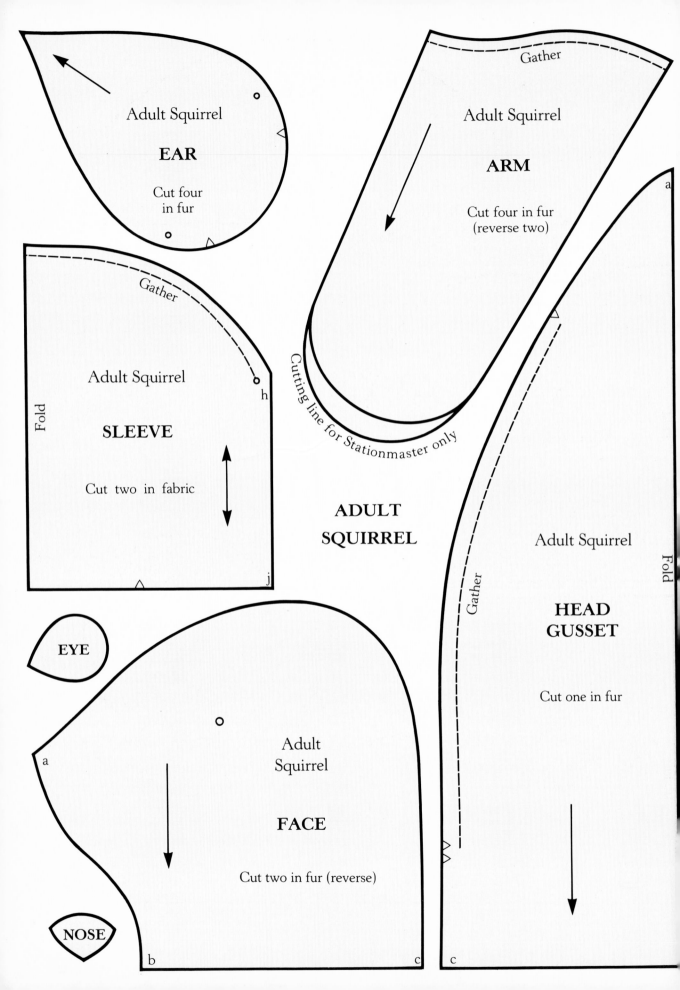

Adult Squirrel

EAR

Cut four
in fur

Adult Squirrel

ARM

Cut four in fur
(reverse two)

Gather

Cutting line for Stationmaster only

Adult Squirrel

SLEEVE

Cut two in fabric

Fold

Gather

ADULT SQUIRREL

Gather

Adult Squirrel

HEAD GUSSET

Cut one in fur

Fold

a

EYE

Adult Squirrel

FACE

Cut two in fur (reverse)

NOSE

a

b

c

c

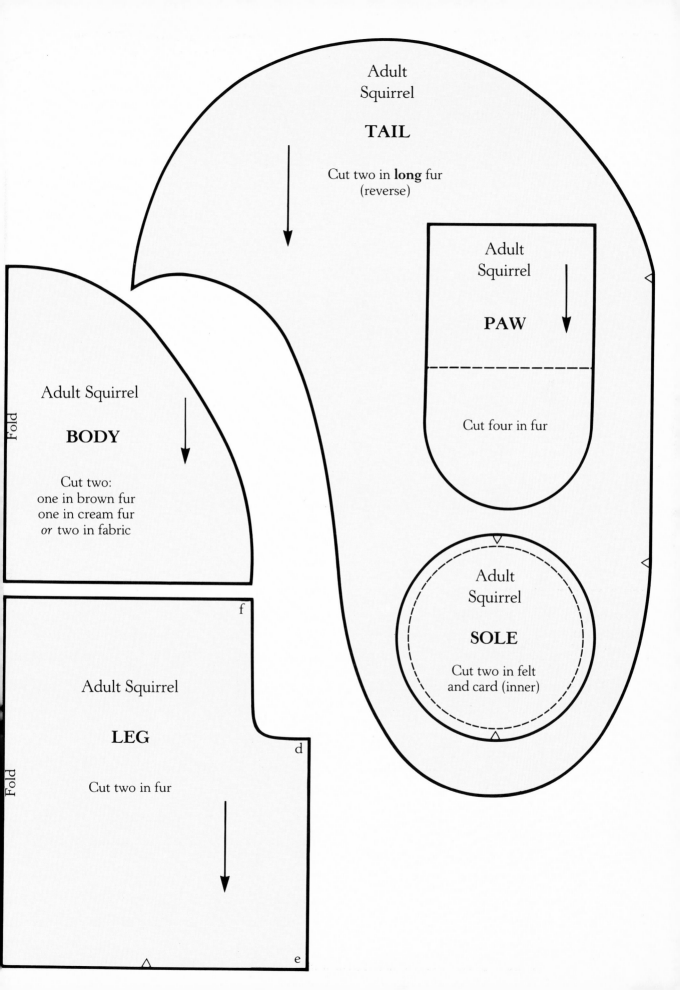

Adult
Squirrel

TAIL

Cut two in **long** fur
(reverse)

Adult
Squirrel

PAW

Cut four in fur

Adult Squirrel

BODY

Cut two:
one in brown fur
one in cream fur
or two in fabric

Fold

Adult
Squirrel

SOLE

Cut two in felt
and card (inner)

Adult Squirrel

LEG

Cut two in fur

Fold

f

d

e

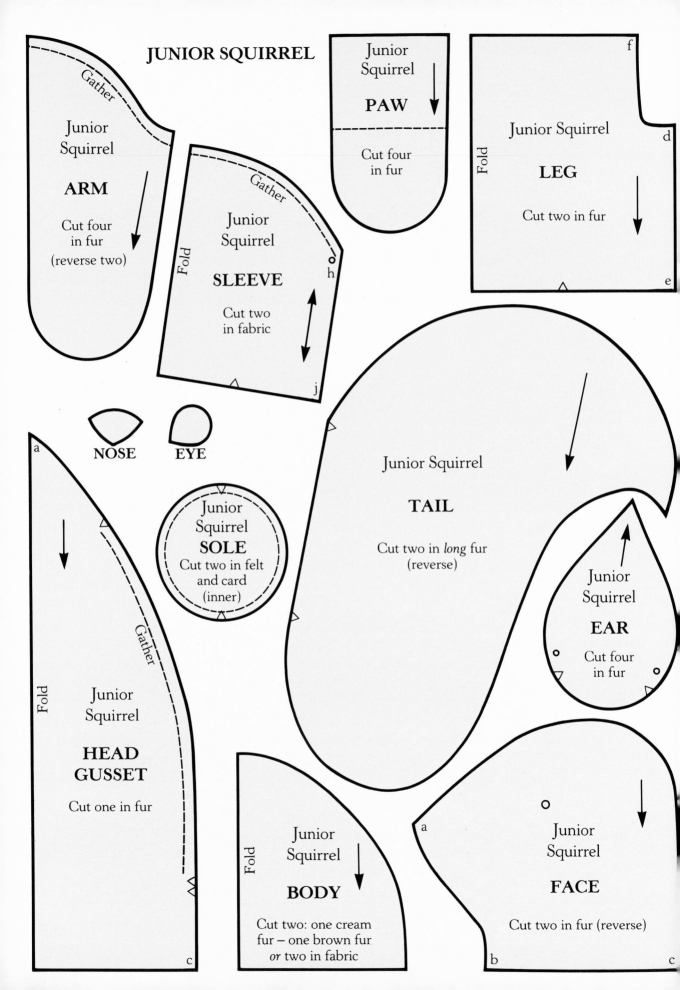

JUNIOR SQUIRREL

Junior
Squirrel

ARM

Cut four
in fur
(reverse two)

Junior
Squirrel

PAW

Cut four
in fur

Junior Squirrel

LEG

Fold

Cut two in fur

Gather

Fold

Junior
Squirrel

SLEEVE

Cut two
in fabric

h

j

NOSE

EYE

a

Junior
Squirrel
SOLE
Cut two in felt
and card
(inner)

Junior Squirrel

TAIL

Cut two in *long* fur
(reverse)

Junior
Squirrel

EAR

Cut four
in fur

Gather

Fold

Junior
Squirrel

**HEAD
GUSSET**

Cut one in fur

Fold

Junior
Squirrel

BODY

Cut two: one cream
fur – one brown fur
or two in fabric

c

a

Junior
Squirrel

FACE

Cut two in fur (reverse)

b

c

THE MOLE

An endearing little creature with a kind and gentle nature, the mole needs a short smooth dark grey fur to emphasise his rounded head and turned-up nose. And although you can use black felt or sequins if you prefer, purchased eyes are best to convey that short-sighted expression.

MATERIALS

25cm (10in) dark grey fur fabric, 80cm (32in) wide (see above)
7 x 14cm (2¾ x 5½in) mid-grey felt for soles
Scrap of black felt
Polyester stuffing
Pair of (purchased) domed black eyes, approx 12mm (½in) diameter, with safety washers
Matching thread
Scraps of stiff card or plastic (double cereal carton or cottage cheese tub lid)
Clear adhesive

SEAM ALLOWANCE

5mm (³/₁₆in)

1. In fur fabric, cut the head gusset once; cut the body, the leg and the head twice each (reversing the pattern to cut the second head); cut the arm four times reversing two pieces.
   Cut the sole twice in felt; then cut it again slightly smaller following the broken line, in card or stiff plastic.
   Mark notches.

2. Mark the eye on each head piece by pushing a pin right through the circle on the pattern and into the fabric beneath; then make a neat hole through the fabric with small pointed scissors.

3. Join the two head pieces between a-b.

4. Carefully fit the tip of the gusset to the end of this seam, matching points a, then join each side to the head between points a-c.

5. Turn to the right side and fit the eyes through the holes; check that they are correctly balanced, then fix the safety washers inside the head.

6. Stuff the head quite firmly, pushing the filling well up into the nose and chin. Using a double thread, gather round the lower edge of the head, then draw up tightly and secure, leaving just a small hole about 2cm (¾in) diameter (before securing your thread, check that the head is sufficiently stuffed, adding a little more filling if it is needed). Mould the head very carefully into shape, following the illustrations for guidance.

7. Now turn to the basic Adult Rabbit (page 100) and follow the directions for the 'all-fur' version, steps 6-12 inclusive.

8. Cut the nose in black felt and glue it over point a, where the tip of the gusset joins the two head pieces.

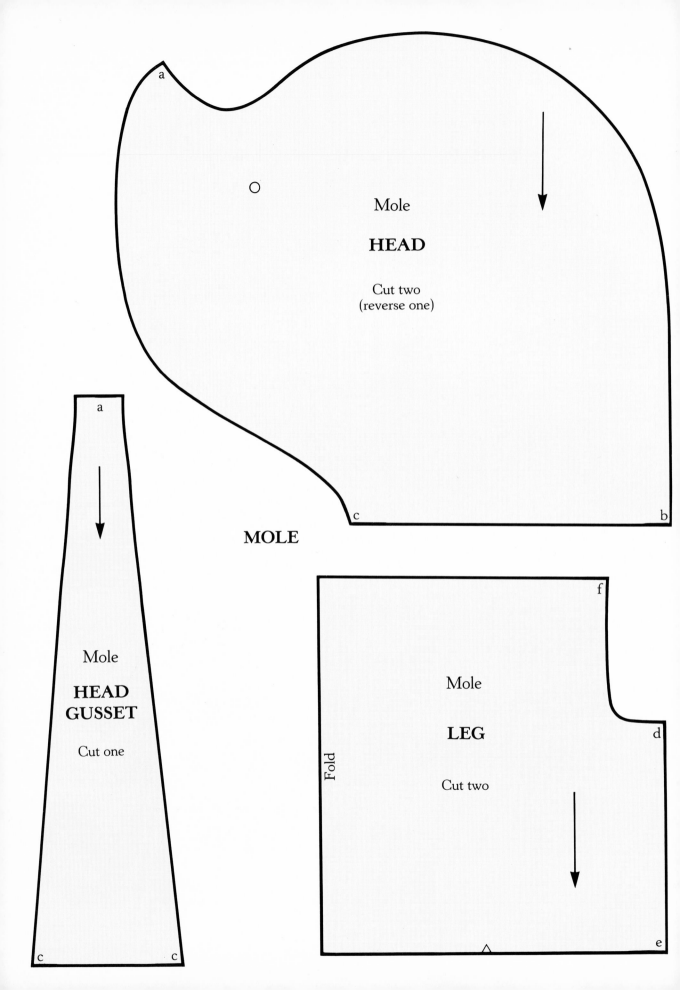

Mole

HEAD

Cut two
(reverse one)

MOLE

Mole

**HEAD
GUSSET**

Cut one

Mole

LEG

Cut two

Fold

a

c b

a

c c

f

d

e

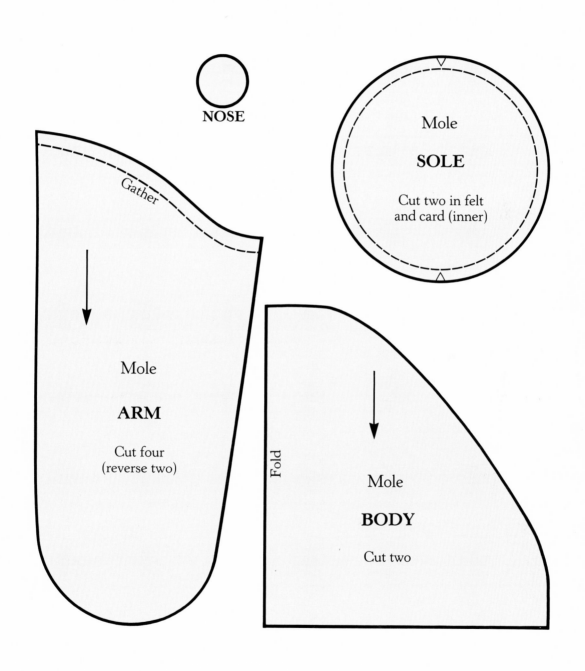

NOSE

Gather

Mole

ARM

Cut four
(reverse two)

Mole

SOLE

Cut two in felt
and card (inner)

Fold

Mole

BODY

Cut two

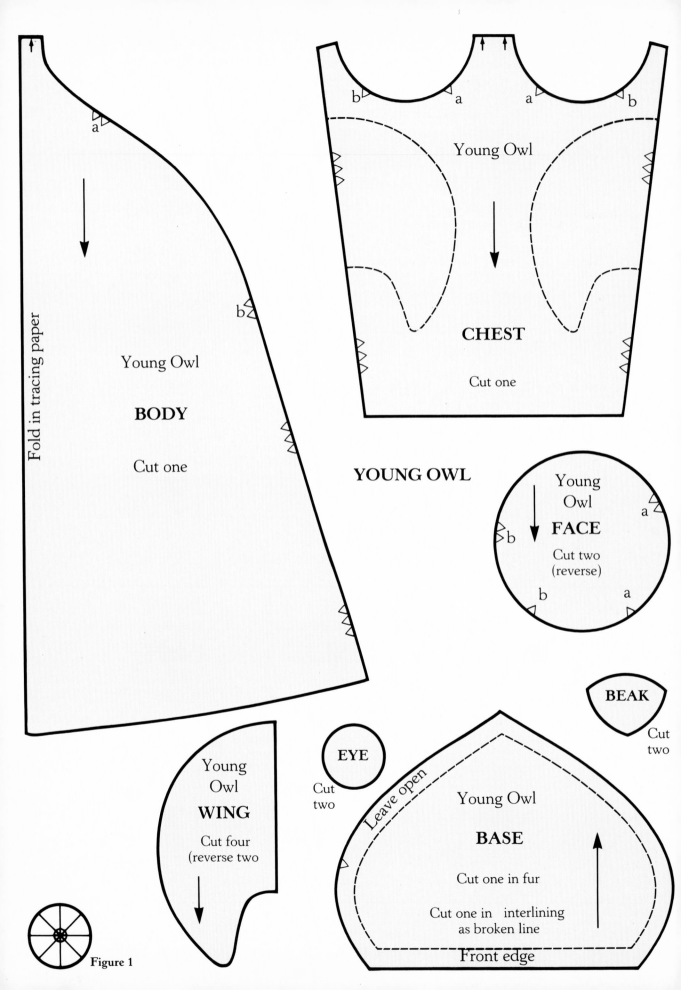

Fold in tracing paper

Young Owl

BODY

Cut one

Young Owl

CHEST

Cut one

YOUNG OWL

b a a b

Young Owl

FACE

Cut two
(reverse)

b a

b a

BEAK

Cut
two

Young
Owl

WING

Cut four
(reverse two

EYE

Cut
two

Leave open

Young Owl

BASE

Cut one in fur

Cut one in interlining
as broken line

Front edge

Figure 1

ADULT, JUNIOR AND BABY OWLS

A very attractive quickie if you are selling your wares. Large, medium and small, all the owls are made in exactly the same way, from a minimum of pattern pieces. Quick to cut out, easy to sew and a dream to stuff, this design also gives you full rein to use your imagination. Be traditional or amusing in your choice of colours, and combine long or short furs for different effects.

As he's still too young to fly, the baby hasn't any wings. And if you're in a hurry, you could omit the young owl's wings too. Otherwise the directions are basically the same. Professor Barnowl is a striking character in dark brown fur with a golden face and cream chest. Whilst Mistress Barnowl creates a much softer effect in camel fur with a cream face and white chest. Even her eyes are a less intense yellow than his, ringed with golden-yellow braid instead of the dark brown which emphasises the headmaster's highly intellectual appearance. And their young students demonstrate in lots more ways the fun you can have when you switch the furs around.

The two adult owls have dark brown pupils, and the same felt is used for the beak. But have a contrasting beak if you prefer — like some of the younger owls in the photograph. The padded beak really is well worth the effort, because it stands away from the face so realistically. But if you want to speed up the production line, glue the two pieces of felt together without any filling between, then stitch it to the head as for the sewn version.

When you have finished, take special care to release all the trapped fur around the eyes, especially on the smaller owls. This gives them that lovely dewy-eyed just-out-of-the-egg appearance which makes them so endearing.

ADULT OWL
MATERIALS
35 x 45cm (14 x 18in) fur fabric for body and wings
23 x 17cm (9 x 6½in) fur fabric for chest
9 x 18cm (3½ x 7in) fur fabric for face
4 x 8cm (1½ x 3in) yellow (or alternative) felt for eyes
1.5 x 3cm (⅝ x 1¼in) felt for pupils ⎫ or use
4cm (1½in) square of felt for beak ⎭ the same

50cm (½yd) narrow braid (or plaited ribbon)
Polyester stuffing
12 x 18cm (4¾ x 7in) heavy-weight non-woven interlining (Vilene or equivalent)
2 large coloured sequins (preferably domed — about 8mm (5/16in) diameter)
4 small black sequins (preferably domed — about 5mm (3/16in) diameter)
Matching and dark brown and black threads
Clear adhesive

JUNIOR OWL
MATERIALS
20 x 30cm (8 x 12in) fur fabric for body and wings
11cm (4½in) square fur fabric for chest
6 x 12cm (2½ x 4¾in) fur fabric for face
2.5 x 5cm (1 x 2in) yellow or green felt for eyes
2.5 x 6cm (1 x 2¼in) felt for beak
Polyester stuffing
7 x 10cm (2¾ x 4in) heavy-weight non-woven interlining (Vilene or equivalent)
2 large black sequins (preferably domed — about 8mm (5/16in) diameter)
Matching and black threads

BABY OWL
MATERIALS
15 x 18cm (6 x 7in) fur fabric for body
8cm (3in) square fur fabric for chest
4.5 x 9cm (1¾ x 3½in) fur fabric for face
2.5 x 5cm (1 x 2in) yellow or green felt for eyes
2 x 4cm (¾ x 1½in) felt for beak
Polyester stuffing
4.5 x 6cm (1¾ x 2½in) heavy-weight non-woven interlining (Vilene or equivalent)
2 small black sequins (preferably domed — about 5mm (3/16in) diameter)
Matching and black threads

SEAM ALLOWANCES
Adult Owl: approximately 5mm (3/16in)
Junior Owl: approximately 4mm (1/8-3/16in)
Baby Owl: approximately 3mm (1/8in)

(continued on page 116)

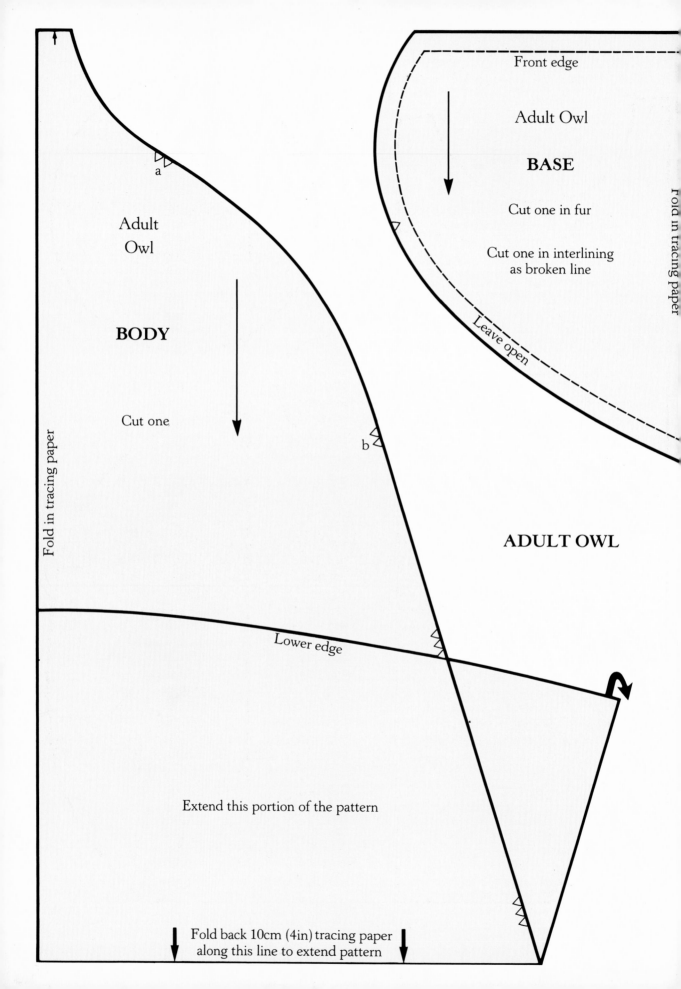

Front edge

Adult Owl

BASE

Cut one in fur

Cut one in interlining
as broken line

Fold in tracing paper

Leave open

Adult
Owl

BODY

Cut one

a

b

Fold in tracing paper

ADULT OWL

Lower edge

Extend this portion of the pattern

Fold back 10cm (4in) tracing paper
along this line to extend pattern

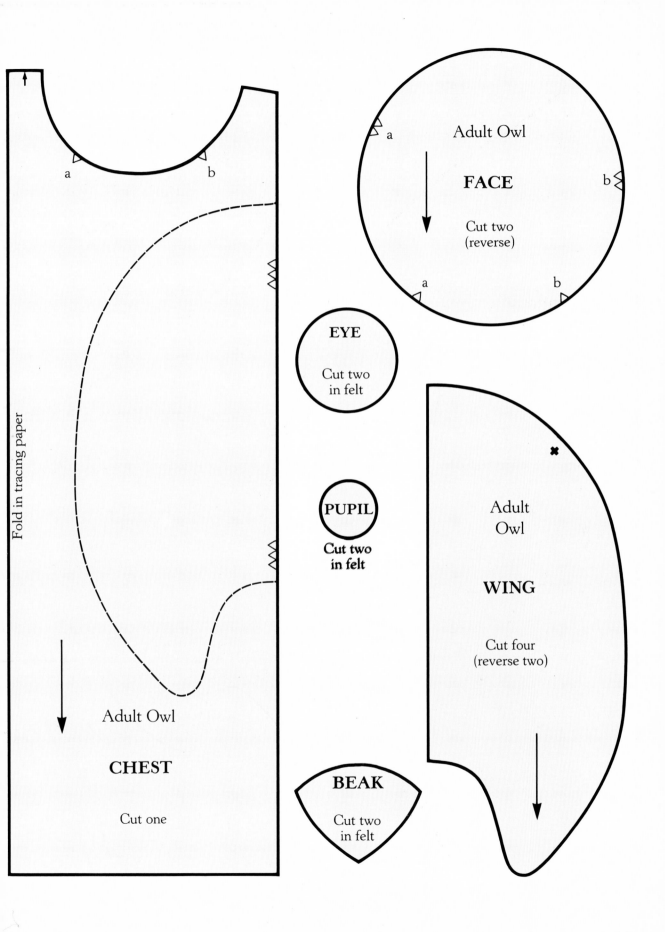

Fold in tracing paper

a　　　　　　　　b

Adult Owl

CHEST

Cut one

a

Adult Owl

FACE

Cut two
(reverse)

b

a　　　　　　　b

EYE

Cut two
in felt

PUPIL

**Cut two
in felt**

x

Adult
Owl

WING

Cut four
(reverse two)

BEAK

Cut two
in felt

1. Cut the body and base once each, and the wing four times (reversing two), in your main fur. Cut the chest once, and the face circle twice, in the appropriate furs. Cut the eye twice in felt. Cut the base again in interlining, slightly smaller as broken line.

Mark the notches carefully; reverse the face pattern to mark notches on the second piece (note a and b).

2. Appliqué each felt eye in the middle of a face circle; check the position is correct *at the back* by pushing a pin through the centre of the eye and then through the centre of the face.

3. *Junior Owl and Baby Owl*: Using black thread, stitch a sequin in the centre of the eye, holding it in place with eight long straight stitches from the central hole of the sequin to the outer edge of the eye to form a star, as figure 1.

Adult Owl: Using dark brown thread, stitch a small sequin in the centre of the eye, holding it in place with eight long straight stitches from the centre of the sequin to the outer edge of the eye to form a star, as figure 1. Glue narrow braid around the outer edge of the eye as figure 2.

4. Join the top point of the body to the top point of the chest (match the small arrows on both pieces).

5. (Ignore this step if you are making the Baby Owl, or if you are making a Junior Owl without wings.)

To make each wing, *oversew* two pieces together, leaving the straight edge open. Turn to the right side. Oversew a wing to each side of the chest, right sides together and straight edges level, as indicated by the broken line on the pattern.

6. Making sure you have the pile of the fur running in exactly the same direction, pin the lower half of the face circles to the chest, matching the single notches a and b; then stitch.

Now pin the side edges of the body to the sides of the chest, lower edges level and matching the triple notches; stitch — then return and stitch the wing again, from the other side.

Finally, pin the upper half of the face circles to the body piece, matching the double notches a and b; stitch, easing the fur fabric round to fit.

Turn to the right side.

7. Cut the beak twice in felt. Leaving the top edge open, buttonhole stitch neatly round the two lower edges. Pad the inside with a tiny bit of stuffing, then oversew the top edge.

Appliqué the top edge over the join between the body and chest overlapping the face at each side.

Turn to the wrong side again.

8. Tack the interlining to the wrong side of the base (make sure your stitches won't show on the right side).

Stitch the straight front edge of the base to the bottom of the chest, then stitch the side and back edges to the body, leaving one side open between the notch and the tail point.

Turn under and tack a narrow hem along each raw edge, then turn to the right side.

9. Stuff the head firmly, moulding it into shape. Stuff the body very thoroughly, but not quite so firmly as the head. Then slip-stitch the edges of the opening together.

10. For the Adult Owl only, cut the pupil twice in felt. Stitch a large sequin, with a small sequin on top, to the pupil as in figure 3. Glue to the eyes as in figure 4.

11. For the Adult Owl only, bring the wings forward slightly so that the tips overlap the chest at each side, then hold each in position by catching point X firmly to the body.

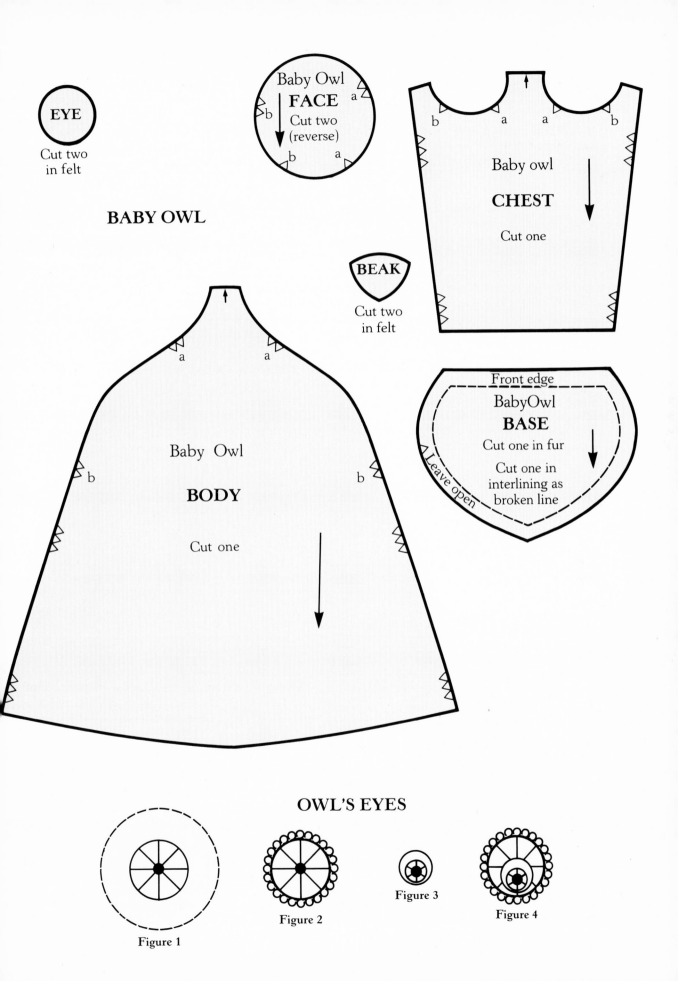

EYE

Cut two
in felt

BABY OWL

Baby Owl
FACE
Cut two
(reverse)

a
b
b   a

Baby owl

CHEST

Cut one

b   a   a   b

BEAK

Cut two
in felt

↑

a   a

b   b

Baby Owl

BODY

Cut one

Front edge

BabyOwl
BASE

Cut one in fur

Cut one in
interlining as
broken line

Leave open

OWL'S EYES

Figure 1

Figure 2

Figure 3

Figure 4

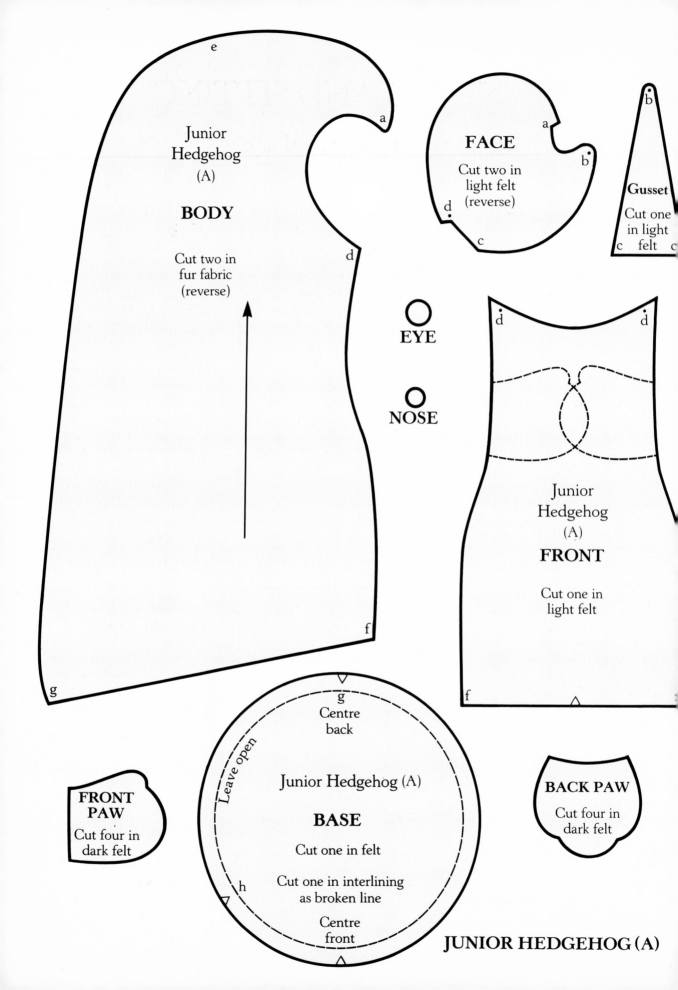

Junior
Hedgehog
(A)

BODY

Cut two in
fur fabric
(reverse)

e

a

d

f

g

FACE

Cut two in
light felt
(reverse)

a

b

d

c

Gusset

Cut one
in light
c   felt   c

b

○
EYE

○
NOSE

d   d

Junior
Hedgehog
(A)

FRONT

Cut one in
light felt

f

Leave open

Centre
back

g

Junior Hedgehog (A)

BASE

Cut one in felt

Cut one in interlining
as broken line

Centre
front

h

**FRONT
PAW**

Cut four in
dark felt

BACK PAW

Cut four in
dark felt

JUNIOR HEDGEHOG (A)

STANDING AND SITTING HEDGEHOGS

Very quick and easy to make — especially the sitting version — and cuddly as can be!

Young or adult, the hedgehog is equally attractive in grey or brown shaggy fur fabric, with toning felts for the face and tummy and the paws. For the brown version, you might prefer to use the darker felt for the base circle.

Just take care matching points a and b, and keep your stitches tiny and very close together when you sew the face and gusset, especially for the smaller hedgehogs. This will ensure you catch that expression of enquiring innocence which has so much to do with this lovable little animal's charm.

THE STANDING HEDGEHOGS

ADULT
MATERIALS
30 x 35cm (12 x 13in) brown-mixture or grey/black-
    mixture fur fabric
18 x 30cm (7 x 12in) beige felt
10 x 20cm (4 x 8in) or a 15cm (6in) square toning brown
    or light grey felt for the paws
Scrap of black felt
11cm (4⅜in) circle heavy-weight non-woven
    interlining (Vilene or equivalent)
Polyester stuffing
Matching threads
Clear adhesive

JUNIOR (A)
MATERIALS
20 x 24cm (8 x 9½in) brown-mixture
    or grey/black-mixture fur fabric
15 x 20cm (6 x 8in) beige felt
10cm (4in) square toning brown or
    light grey for the paws
Scrap of black felt
7cm (2¾in) circle heavy-weight non-woven interlining
    (Vilene or equivalent)
Polyester stuffing
Matching threads
Clear adhesive

SEAM ALLOWANCES (ON FUR FABRIC)
5mm (³/₁₆in) for the Adult — slightly less for the Junior
    version

1. Cut the body twice in fur fabric (reversing the second piece). Cut the gusset, the front and the base once each, and the face twice (reversing the second piece) in beige felt. Cut the paws twice each in brown or grey felt, then pin the cut pieces to the remaining felt and cut again; leave pinned together.
   Cut the base again in interlining, slightly smaller, following the broken line.

2. Prepare each paw by top-stitching quite close to the edge, leaving the back edges open. Pad with a little stuffing, pushing it towards the front half of the paw.

3. Oversew the face pieces together between a-b. Carefully fit the tip of the gusset between the two pieces, matching points b; oversew each side to the face between b-c.

4. Oversew the top of the front to the face between d-d.

5. Place the front paws on the right side of the front piece, positioned exactly as indicated on the pattern. Tack together along the cut edges.

6. With the two body pieces right sides together, join the head between a-e.

7. Open out both the top of the face and front of the head, then place them right sides together with the seams exactly level, and join points a very securely.
   Now pin one side of the face to the body between points a-d, slightly stretching the fur fabric to fit; stitch. Continue down each side of the front, stitching it to the body between d-f.
   Join the other side of the face and front to the body in the same way.

8. Join the centre back seam of the body between e-g.

9. Oversew the back paws to each side of the lower
(continued on page 122)

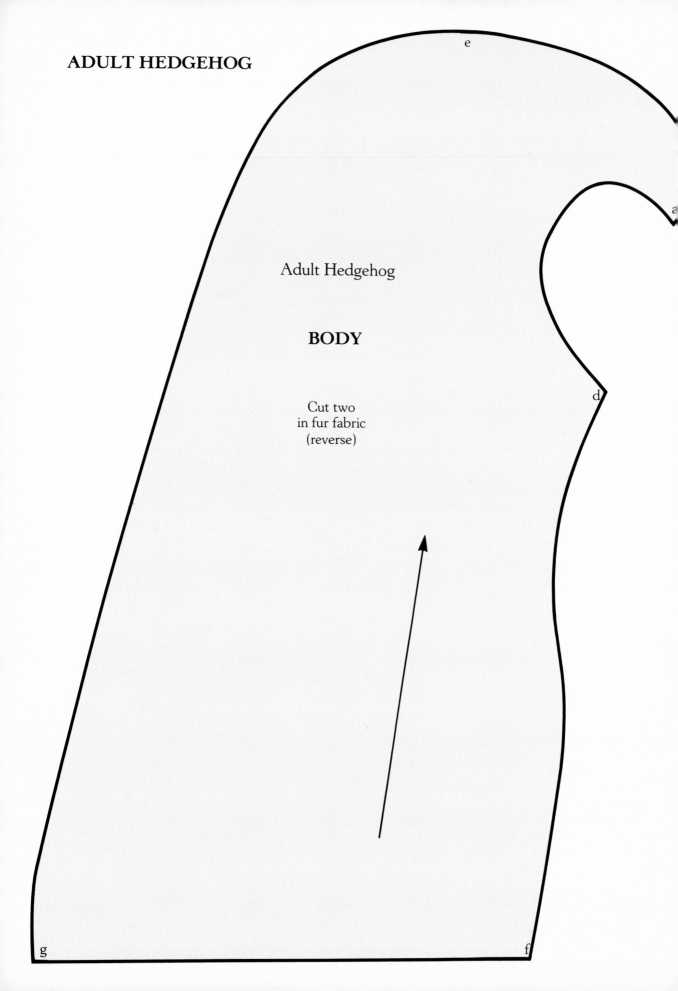

ADULT HEDGEHOG

Adult Hedgehog

BODY

Cut two
in fur fabric
(reverse)

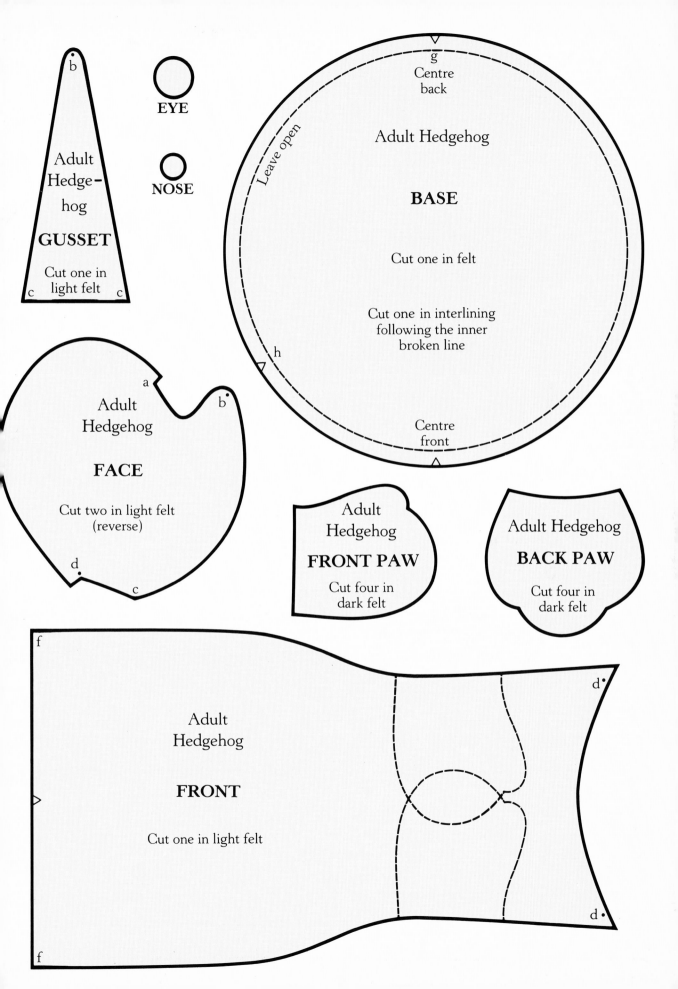

Adult Hedge-hog
GUSSET
Cut one in light felt

b
c   c

EYE

NOSE

Adult Hedgehog
BASE
Cut one in felt
Cut one in interlining following the inner broken line

Centre back
g

Leave open

h

Centre front

Adult Hedgehog
FACE
Cut two in light felt (reverse)

a
b
d   c

Adult Hedgehog
FRONT PAW
Cut four in dark felt

Adult Hedgehog
BACK PAW
Cut four in dark felt

f

Adult Hedgehog
FRONT
Cut one in light felt

d

f   d

edge of the front, right sides together and cut edges level, as for the front paws; have the outer edge of each paw against the seam at f.

10. Tack the interlining to the wrong side of the base, centres matching.

Pin the base to the lower edge of the hedgehog, then stitch, leaving one side open between the notches as indicated. Turn under a narrow hem at each side of the opening, then turn to the right side.

11. Stuff the head very carefully, beginning by pushing a tiny bit of filling right up into the point of the nose. Gradually add more filling until the nose is very firmly filled and a good shape. Continue to stuff the face, pushing the filling forward from the back, finally stuffing the rest of the head.

Stuff the body very well, but not as firmly as head. Then stitch edges of opening neatly together.

12. Cut the eyes and nose in black felt (see Creating Character — cutting circles: page 7). Glue the nose circle to the face over point b. Pin the eyes to the face, following the illustration and moving them around until you like the expression, then glue into position.

THE SITTING HEDGEHOGS

JUNIOR (B)
MATERIALS
12 x 30cm (5 x 12in) brown-mixture or
    grey/black-mixture fur fabric
15cm (6in) square beige felt
Scrap of black felt
8 x 10cm (3 x 4in) heavy-weight non-woven interlining
    (Vilene or equivalent)
Polyester stuffing
Matching threads
Clear adhesive

BABY
MATERIALS
9 x 20cm (3½ x 8in) brown-mixture or grey/black-
    mixture fur fabric
10cm (4in) square beige felt
Scrap of black felt
5cm x 6cm (2 x 2½in) heavy-weight non-woven interlining
    (Vilene or equivalent)
Polyester stuffing
Matching threads
Clear adhesive

SEAM ALLOWANCES (ON FUR FABRIC)
Just under 5mm (³⁄₁₆in) for the Junior Hedgehog —
    3mm (⅛in) for the Baby

1. Cut the body twice in fur fabric (reversing the second piece). Cut the gusset and the base once each, and the face twice (reversing the second piece) in beige felt.

Cut the base again in interlining, slightly smaller, following the broken line.

2. Oversew the face pieces together between a-b. Carefully fit the tip of the gusset between the two pieces, matching points b; oversew each side to the face between b-c.

3. With the two body pieces right sides together, join the head between a-d.

4. Open out both the top of the face and front of the head, then place them right sides together with the seams exactly level, and join points a very securely.

Now pin one side of the face to the body between points a-e, slightly stretching the fur fabric to fit; stitch.

Join the other side of the face to the body in the same way.

5. Join the centre back seam of the body between d-f.

6. Tack the interlining to the wrong side of the base.

Pin the base to the lower edge of the hedgehog, matching centre front and back points to the seams at g and f, then stitch, leaving open between the notches as indicated. Turn under a narrow hem at each side of the opening, then turn to the right side.

7. Stuff the head very carefully, beginning by pushing a tiny bit of filling right up into the point of the nose; gradually add more filling until the nose is very firmly filled and a good shape. Continue to stuff the face, pushing the filling forward from the back, finally stuffing the rest of the body; stuff the body well, but not as firmly as the head. Then stitch the edges of the opening neatly together.

8. Cut the eyes and nose in black felt (see Creating Character — cutting circles: page 7. Use a hole punch, if you have one, for tiny circles). Glue the nose circle to the face over point b. Pin the eyes to the face, following the illustration and moving them around until you are satisfied with the expression, then glue into position.

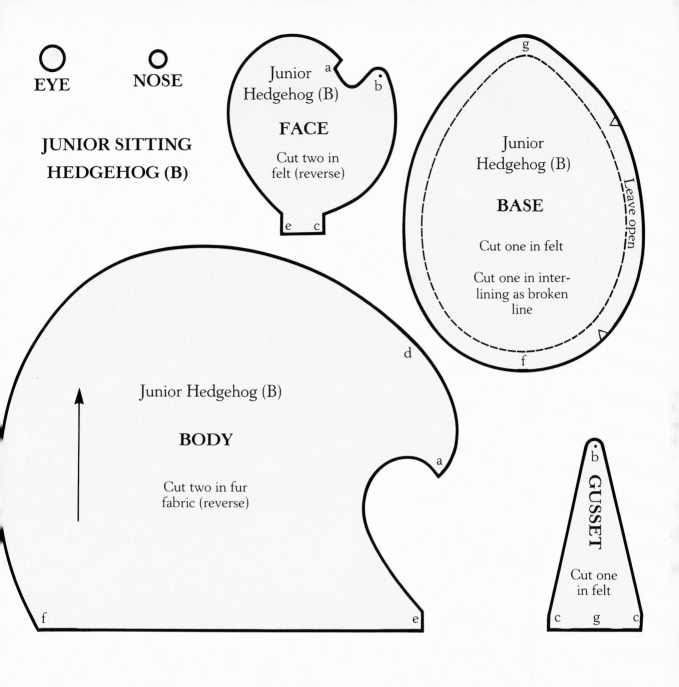

EYE

NOSE

JUNIOR SITTING
HEDGEHOG (B)

Junior
Hedgehog (B)

FACE

Cut two in
felt (reverse)

a

b

e   c

Junior
Hedgehog (B)

BASE

Cut one in felt

Cut one in inter-
lining as broken
line

g

Leave open

f

Junior Hedgehog (B)

BODY

Cut two in fur
fabric (reverse)

d

a

f   e

b

GUSSET

Cut one
in felt

c   g   c

BABY SITTING HEDGEHOG

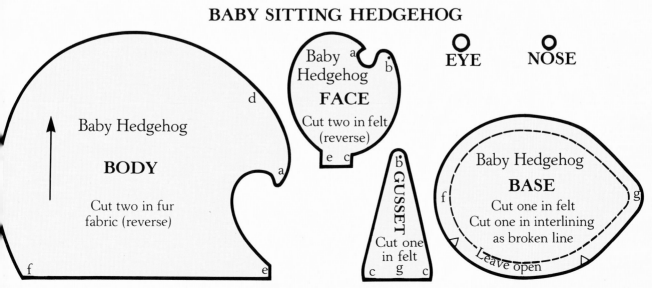

Baby Hedgehog

BODY

Cut two in fur
fabric (reverse)

d

a

f   e

Baby
Hedgehog

FACE

Cut two in felt
(reverse)

a

b

e   c

EYE

NOSE

b

GUSSET

Cut one
in felt

c   g   c

Baby Hedgehog

BASE

Cut one in felt

Cut one in interlining
as broken line

f   g

Leave open

THE BLACKBERRY

HOLLOW PIXIES

Every community has its problems. And the residents of Blackberry Hollow are no exception. In their case it's the pixies. The animals are really quite fond of them; but they do wish the pixies would stay at home in their toadstool and not bother everyone quite so much. Because whenever the pixies offer to help, trouble is never far behind.

But from your point of view, the pixies are nothing but good news. They are amusing, versatile little characters, full of animation, quick, easy and inexpensive to make. Best of all, they are a gift for anyone who needs a mascot (and who doesn't!).

Have fun choosing seasonal shades for their colour co-ordinated outfits. Study the photographs for guidance in developing your own ideas. Embroidery wool or fine knitting yarn is used for the hair, but if you haven't anything lightweight it won't matter if you substitute a heavier yarn; just decrease the number of strands according to the thickness.

MATERIALS
20cm (8in) square cream felt
10 x 16cm (4 x 6½in) felt for legs
15 x 16cm (6 x 6½in) felt for tunic
18 x 10cm (7 x 4in) felt for hat
   or 18cm (7in) square felt for legs and hat
   or 20cm (8in) square felt for tunic and hat
Scrap of black felt for eyes
2 pipe cleaners (chenille stems) 16.5cm (6½in) long
Polyester stuffing
Twilley's stranded embroidery wool for hair (or 3-ply
   knitting yarn)
Pinky-red stranded embroidery cotton
Matching and black sewing threads
Scrap of stiff card (cereal carton)
Clear adhesive

1. In cream felt, cut the front head and the neck and the arms once each; cut the back head and body twice each; cut the hand twice, then pin each piece to the remaining felt and cut again — leave pinned together. In the appropriate colours, cut the hat and tunic once each, and the sleeve, leg and sole twice each. Cut the inner sole twice in card.

2. For the NECK bend a pipe cleaner in half; then bend it in half again (figure 1a). Place at one side of the felt (figure 1b), then wind the felt tightly round the pipe cleaner and slip-stitch the join (figure 1c).

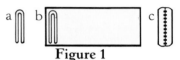
Figure 1

3. For the ARMS bend the ends of the second pipe cleaner under so that it measures 13cm (5⅛in) (figure 2a). Glue along the top edge of the arm felt (figure 2b); then roll tightly round and glue the join (figure 2c).

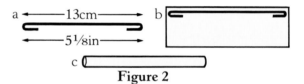
Figure 2

4. Oversew round the HANDS, leaving the straight edges open; make tiny stitches, close together. Push a tiny bit of stuffing down into the tip of each, then fit it on the end of the pipe cleaner (figure 3a). Bind the wrists tightly with thread as indicated on the pattern, and secure (figure 3b). Then gather the straight top edge and draw up neatly around the arm (figure 3c).

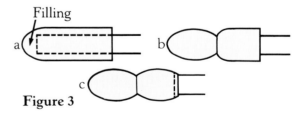
Figure 3

5. Join the back pieces of the HEAD for centre back seam a-b, leaving open between the notches (figure 4a). Open out and join to the front circle (figure 4b), matching points a and b, and leaving open at the base between the notches.

Turn to the right side; place neck inside and push down through the base slit until only 5mm (¼in) remains inside the head. Make sure the neck join is at

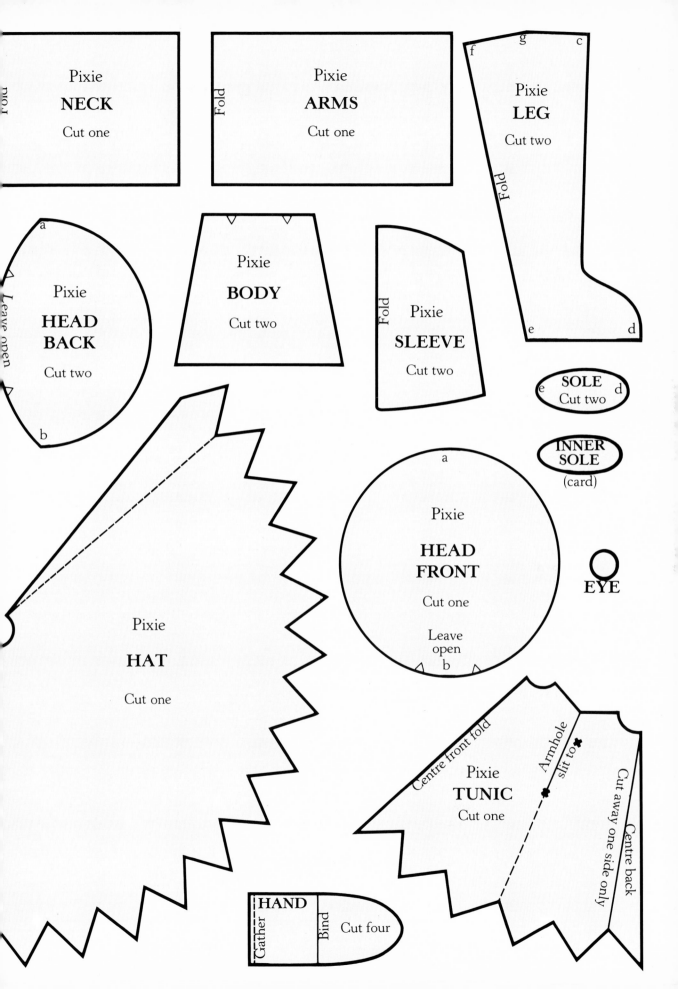

the back, then stitch the edge of the head neatly around the neck (figure 4c).

Stuff the head very firmly, moulding to shape, then close and stitch centre back seam.

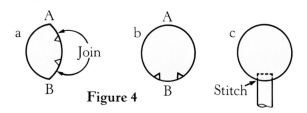

Figure 4

6. Mark the centre point of the arms, then place them *behind* the neck, palms down, 1cm (⅜in) below the head (figure 5); stitch securely, oversewing each right-angle.

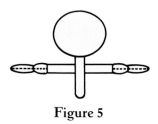

Figure 5

7. Join the BODY pieces at *one* shoulder only, between the corner and the notch. Place around the neck and then join the other shoulder. Stitch around the neck. Bring down tightly over the arms, then catch together underneath and join the side seams (figure 6).

Stuff well, keeping the neck piece in the centre, then join the lower edges.

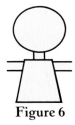

Figure 6

8. For each LEG join the centre front seam c-d. Pin the sole around he lower edge, matching points d and e; stitch (figure 7a). Turn to the right side. Fit the card inner sole inside the foot (anchor from outside with a pin). Stuff very firmly, pushing a little filling well down into the foot and then continuing up to the top of the leg, using only a small amount at a time.

Close the top edge by folding at points g, matching c-f (figure 7b). Join close to the top edge with a gathering stitch; draw up to measure about 2cm (¾in) and secure (figure 7c).

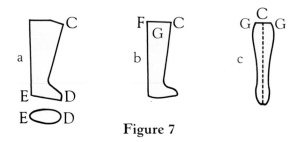

Figure 7

9. Stitch the top edge of the legs to the lower edge of the body, matching outer point g on each leg to the corner of the body (figure 8): place front of leg against front of body to oversew together from the back.

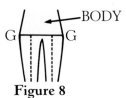

Figure 8

10. Fold the TUNIC along the broken lines below the armhole slits, then join the front to the back at the shoulders (figure 9).

Join the side seam of each sleeve, then set into the armholes, matching the centre of the top edge to the shoulder seam, and the sleeve seam to the bottom of the slit in the tunic.

Fit on the figure and overlap the back edges, cutting away one side only as indicated on the pattern; slip-stitch together.

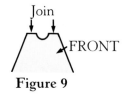

Figure 9

11. For the HAIR, cut sixty 14cm (5½in) lengths of yarn (fewer if you are using thicker yarn). If you are not using strands of wool cut a 14cm (5½in) deep piece of card and wind yarn evenly round it thirty times, then cut neatly along both edges (figure 10). Place the strands of yarn over the top of the head, across the seam, hanging down at front and back;

Figure 10

126

catch securely into place with matching thread, to cover 3cm (1¼in) of the seam.

Cut forty 18cm (7in) lengths of yarn. Place them across the first strands, to hang down evenly at each side; catch tightly to centre top of head, over the seam.

Arrange the strands evenly around the head, then spread a little glue underneath and press them down lightly to hold in position.

12. Overlap the straight edges of the HAT as broken line on pattern; pin join and try on pixie's head to check fit. Adjust if necessary, then stitch or glue the join.

Spread a little glue inside, then fix on the pixie's head, seam at back.

13. Trim the hair neatly to length all round (figure 11), following the illustrations.

14. Cut the eyes in black felt (see Creating Character — cutting circles: page 7); pin to the face about 2cm (¾in) apart (figure 12).

Using black sewing thread, embroider the nose with two tiny straight stitches, one on top of the other; position it level with the lower edge of the eyes (figure 12).

Using two strands of embroidery cotton, work the mouth in stem or outline stitch, about 1cm (⅜in) wide (or slightly more for a broader grin), and 6-7mm (¼in) below the nose (figure 12).

Check you are still satisfied with the position of the eyes, then glue into place.

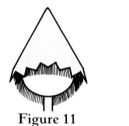

Figure 11

2cm (¾in)

Figure 12

INDEX